Research in Criminology

Series Editors
Alfred Blumstein
David P. Farrington

Research in Criminology

Paul B. Paulus

Prison Crowding:
A Psychological Perspective

With the collaboration of Verne C. Cox and Garvin McCain

With 12 Illustrations

Springer-Verlag
New York Berlin Heidelberg
London Paris Tokyo

Paul B. Paulus
Department of Psychology, University of Texas at Arlington, Arlington, Texas
76019-0528, USA

Series Editors
Alfred Blumstein
School of Urban and Public Affairs, Carnegie-Mellon University, Pittsburgh,
Pennsylvania 15213, USA

David P. Farrington
Institute of Criminology, University of Cambridge, Cambridge,
CB3 9DT, England

Library of Congress Cataloging-in-Publication Data
Paulus, Paul B.
  Prison crowding.
  (Research in criminology)
  Bibliography: p.
  1. Prison psychology. 2. Prisons—Overcrowding—
Psychological aspects. 3. Crowding stress. 4. Prisons—
United States—Overcrowding. I. Cox, Verne C., 1938–
II. McCain, Garvin, 1922– . III. Title. IV. Series.
HV6089.P38 1988   365'.64   87-28670

Typeset by Asco Trade Typesetting Ltd, Hong Kong.
Printed and bound by R.R. Donnelley & Sons, Harrisonburg, Virginia.
Printed in the United States of America.

9 8 7 6 5 4 3 2 1

ISBN 0-387-96650-1 Springer-Verlag New York Berlin Heidelberg
ISBN 3-540-96650-1 Springer-Verlag Berlin Heidelberg New York

To all who made this research possible:
the inmates, the correctional personnel and officials,
the research assistants and associates,
and my patient and tolerant family.

Preface

This volume is a summary of a 15-year effort to determine the effects of prison crowding and their relationship to the broader realm of crowding phenomena and theories. Although the writing of this volume was for the most part a solitary effort, the data and ideas it is based on were mostly the result of a collaborative effort with Verne Cox and Garvin McCain. Their schedules limited their ability to contribute to this volume, but they provided much constructive feedback and assistance. Cox also wrote a preliminary draft of Chapter 3, and both McCain and Cox made major contributions to Chapter 5 and assisted with several other chapters. I am greatly indebted to these two fine scholars for their efforts and support over the course of our joint research endeavors. In recognition of this fact, the pronoun "we" is used throughout this volume.

This research would not have been possible without the cooperation and support of thousands of inmates and hundreds of prison officials. The unconditional support throughout the project from Director Norman Carlson and former regional research director Jerome Mabli, both of the Federal Bureau of Prisons, is also greatly appreciated. Thanks are due to the National Institute of Justice for financial support during various phases of this project. The support of John Spevacek of the Institute was indispensable. Funds were also provided by the Hogg Foundation, U.S. Department of Justice–Civil Rights Division, and the University of Texas at Arlington.

A Visiting Fellowship Award from the National Institute of Justice provided the time and resources necessary to complete the data acquisition and the extensive analyses on which much of this volume is based. Patrick Langan of the Institute was a superb host during that time. Marc Schaeffer provided invaluable assistance in data management and analysis, and Gerald Gaes (U.S. Bureau of Prisons) provided statistical guidance during the Visiting Fellowship period and collaborated in several studies. The Uniformed Services University of the Health Sciences, Department of Medical Psychology, provided an "intellectual home" and much ancillary support. Andrew Baum was instrumental in making the Visiting Fellowship year a rewarding one, both professionally and personally.

In presenting the results of our many research endeavors, an attempt was made not to overwhelm the reader with statistical details. Many of these details can be found in the various reports and publications cited in this volume. The main purpose was to provide a broad psychological perspective on the issue of prison crowding that would be of benefit to both scholars and criminal justice professionals.

Paul B. Paulus

Contents

1
Introduction

This is a book about prisons and about crowding. Most of the research to be discussed was conducted in prisons and is of use in resolving basic questions about prison design and housing. However, the aim in this research was not to understand prisons per se, but the nature and consequences of living in crowded conditions. This was a major concern of a wide array of researchers when we first began our studies. The choice of prisons as a site for research was predicated on a variety of methodological and conceptual grounds. It was felt that characteristics of living conditions in many prisons provided a unique opportunity to examine a variety of issues in the area of crowding. Even though the aim was "basic" research, the research in prisons soon led to involvement in a number of legal battles about the constitutionality of living conditions in prisons. This forced my colleagues and me to address the practical implications of our work as well as its theoretical meaning. In fact, the pressures of carrying out the research and being involved in the various legal proceedings made it difficult to find time for reflective theoretical appraisal of our results. This book represents an attempt to incorporate in one volume the empirical, theoretical, and practical fruits of a 15-year effort. The story is by no means complete. Many empirical, theoretical, and practical questions remain. Yet this work and that of others have at least provided an outline for future endeavors in this area. It is hoped that this outline will stimulate other scholars to fill in many of the gaps that remain.

When this project began in 1970, psychologists were just becoming seriously interested in the issue of crowding. A scattering of sociological studies had existed for some time, but it was a study by Calhoun with rodents that stimulated social and environmental psychologists to action. Calhoun (1962) studied rodents living in crowded conditions and found evidence of disturbances in sexual and maternal behavior as well as increased aggressive behavior and enhanced mortality. Similar results were obtained in other studies with animals (Christian & Davis, 1964), and psychologists began to wonder whether humans might be similarly affected by living in high density conditions. To assess effects of high density conditions in humans, a large series of experimental studies were done. These involved confining small groups of individuals under conditions that varied in spaciousness and size of the group. Some studies found little evidence of negative effects (Freedman, 1975), but others found that temporary conditions of crowding can produce negative feelings and decrements in task performance (Paulus, 1980). While these studies are pertinent for evaluating reactions to short-term and temporary conditions of crowding, they may be of little help in understanding what happens when people live in crowded conditions for long periods of time.

To study real-world, long-term crowding, sociologists had been examining statistics for people living in areas of cities that varied in degree of crowding. Some of these studies obtained dramatic evidence that crowded city living can have detrimental effects on health and the level of socially disruptive behavior (Galle, Gove, & McPherson, 1972). Yet others failed to obtain such dramatic findings (Freedman, Heshka, & Levy, 1975), and this type of research was subjected to criticism on a variety of methodological and statistical grounds (Kirmeyer, 1978). One of the major problems with this research was the fact that people in cities have some degree of choice as to where they live. Thus, it is possible that people who choose to live in or tolerate living in crowded parts of cities are different from those who live in less crowded areas. Also, socioeconomic factors are so closely intertwined with crowding in cities that it may be impossible to separate the effects of each.

To overcome the problems inherent in the laboratory and city studies, some investigators began looking for environments where individuals were housed under crowded conditions for extended periods of time, but did not have a choice as to where they lived. The college dormitory was one environment that met these criteria and was the subject of many interesting and successful studies demonstrating a wide variety of effects of crowded living conditions. However, the crowding experienced in college dormitories is still relatively mild compared with that experienced in other sectors of our society. With all of these considerations in mind, Verne Cox, Garvin McCain, and I surveyed a wide variety of possibilities—homes for aged veterans, offshore oil rigs, junior high schools, apartment complexes, jails, and prisons. Although each of these environments had some features of interest, we were most impressed with the potential of research in prisons. We discovered that prisons come in a wide variety of sizes and shapes. Although we found a number of "classic" prisons that housed inmates in long corridors of small cells, other prisons housed inmates in a broad range of housing types—singles, doubles, multiple-occupant cells with three to nine inmates, open dormitories with 20 to 150 inmates, and dormitories where space was broken up into small segments or individual cubicles.

The amount of space available also varied greatly among the housing types. While some prisons housed a large number of inmates, others were comparatively small. We quickly realized that prisons provided us with an opportunity to examine a wide variety of aspects of crowded living—the number of people in one's housing unit, the amount of available space, and the population density of the general residential area. Furthermore, in most cases, inmates cannot choose their prison or their living quarters within the prison. They are assigned to their housing by administrative personnel using a wide variety of criteria: nature of the crime, previous criminal history, length of confinement in prison, work or program assignment, etc. Although lack of inmate control over housing assignment overcomes the self-selection problem, the assignment policies may result in different types of inmates being assigned to different types of housing. We dealt with this problem by searching for prisons where this was not the case or where the impact of assignment policy could be evaluated independent of housing type.

One feature of prisons that makes them attractive is the fact that the level of crowding that is found in some prisons is much greater than typically found in the free world. In some cases inmates are housed around the clock in units with 50 or more inmates and less than 20 sq ft of space per person. To approximate this level of crowding in a 1,000 sq ft apartment, it would have to contain 50 or more residents. This would certainly violate community safety codes and be an intolerable situation for its residents. Yet these types of conditions are encountered frequently in prisons and jails.

Although prisons have many characteristics that make them attractive to crowding researchers, they are not without drawbacks as research sites. Probably one such drawback that keeps most researchers away is that they are generally unpleasant and depressing places to visit. They tend to be located in out-of-the-way places, and the atmosphere of tension in prisons and the ever-present danger have taken a toll on our nerves on a number of occasions. In the federal prison system, personnel receive early retirement because they are considered to be on dangerous duty. Yet most federal prisons do not approach the level of tension and violence found in state prisons.

The mechanics of research in prisons are also quite different from those required to do research in other more benign environments. A major part of the process is finding suitable research sites. We consulted various sources that list prisons and their characteristics to locate potential sites of interest. We sought prisons that had a broad range of housing types. Prisons that had primarily one type of housing were eliminated. Initially, we focused on prisons within driving distance, but later funds from a variety of sources allowed us to consider sites in the entire United States.

Once we located prisons of interest, we attempted to get more detailed information from the officials at the prisons. This involved telephone interviews and requests for reports and copies of blueprints. Those prisons that passed this stage were visited to examine the housing in detail, determine the housing assignment policy, and assess the feasibility of conducting research.

There were two major impediments to our research efforts. The initial work was funded by small sums from our university, but many expenses had to be defrayed by the investigators. This situation was not conducive to an all-out effort. The National Science Foundation turned down a grant proposal due in part to our lack of experience in doing this research. Ironically, at that time, no one else had this experience either. After some initial studies, funding was obtained from the National Institute of Justice for a more comprehensive project. Another problem was getting permission to do research in prisons. This turned out to be no problem at all for the federal prison system since we received strong support from Director Norman Carlson and other officials. They seemed quite interested in learning about the importance of housing in adjustment to prison life. Yet, approval at this level was not sufficient. We still had to elicit cooperation from the wardens and personnel at each potential prison site. Although we were often viewed with some skepticism initially, we inevitably received full cooperation and support. Of course, we still had to convince inmates to participate in the study. This turned out to be the easiest task of all. Most of the inmates were more than happy to participate in a project that might lead to an improvement in their living conditions or provide a break in their dull routine.

At the level of state prisons, cooperation was another matter. Although we made valiant efforts to launch research in a number of state systems, our efforts were thwarted at high levels because of the fear that our research findings might be used in a court of law against the system. The federal prison system apparently was not terribly worried about this, since it was part of the judicial agency involved in most of the court actions against the states. Ironically, later we were able to gather data from several state prisons as a result of our involvement as expert witnesses in a wide variety of cases.

We also found a number of jails that had an interesting variety of housing. In contrast to state prison officials, jail officials were most cooperative in allowing us access to their institutions for research. Since legal proceedings against jails because of overcrowding have been relatively few in number, jail administrators may be less concerned about the potentially adverse impact of our work.

When we began our research in prisons, we had very little idea as to what to expect. The literature at that time was rather confusing and inconsistent, and detailed studies of individuals living in crowded housing were nonexistent. Given the adaptive capacities often attributed to humans, it was possible that inmates in crowded prisons would simply adjust to their unpleasant surroundings. Although Freedman (1975) championed this type of perspective, no one had examined individuals crowded under conditions as extreme as those found in prisons.

A second question that intrigued us was the relative importance of the amount of space and the number of people in determining housing satisfaction and their impact on health. Most studies had not clearly separated these two factors. Crowding usually involved many people in little space. Yet which of these two factors is important? Prison standards and court cases tended to focus primarily on space per inmate in determining adequacy of housing. Having to contend with many people in one's housing unit might be an important factor as well. To shed light on this issue, we tried to find prisons where the number of people in a housing unit and the amount of space were somewhat independent and an assessment of their separate effects was feasible.

We anticipated that inmates should be unhappy about living in crowded quarters. Yet, a demonstration of this simple fact would have little scientific or societal significance. If crowding really was a significant source of discomfort and stress for inmates, it should have an impact on the health and behavior of inmates. To determine this, we decided to obtain information about inmate visits to the medical clinics and assess their behavior and physiological state in various ways (e.g., blood pressure). Some potentially severe effects of crowding on health and inmate adjustment (e.g., natural deaths and violence) may be of relatively low frequency and require information on large numbers of inmates. So whenever possible, we obtained institutional records about levels of crowding and the incidence of mortality, violence, and psychiatric commitments.

In considering the various features of the different types of housing, we wondered to what extent such features as windows, hallway length, degree of visual privacy, availability of recreational or lounge areas, single versus double bunking, and private versus shared toilets were related to housing satisfaction. Several opportunities to examine the impact of such housing characteristics did arise.

We did not begin our work with strong theoretical ideas or inclinations. We felt that theoretical efforts were premature, given the paucity of data. Accordingly, we resolved to have the data lead us in the path of theory development. We did, however, have some vague theoretical biases. It seemed to us that having to deal with others in a limited housing area was likely to be a more significant problem than the amount of space available—space can't "bite," but people can. We also expected that individuals who lived under crowded conditions for an extended length of time would become somewhat tolerant of these conditions and react less negatively. Thus, throughout our research program, we endeavored to assess crowding tolerance independent of other psychological and health-related reactions.

Although our motivation in doing this research was primarily that of basic empirical science, we were not insensitive to its pragmatic potential. Court cases contesting crowded conditions in prisons were increasing in number, and our findings would prove to have a bearing on these cases and standards for prison design. We did not anticipate the eventual degree of impact. Not only has our work been cited in numerous cases at all levels of the judiciary, but our personal expertise was sought in many of these cases, including the U.S. Supreme Court. The U.S. Justice Department solicited our assistance in a wide variety of cases and funded various projects to gather more evidence. Public attention was drawn to our work by national television, newspapers, and magazines. Our findings have been the basis for system-wide changes in housing standards and will be used in formulating new public health standards for prisons.

The practical fallout from our work is certainly gratifying. Yet, it is felt that the empirical and theoretical fruits of our work are quite significant in themselves. This volume will present the major results of our studies and our theoretical efforts. This work is of potential significance to a wide variety of disciplines—social psychology, sociology, environmental psychology, and criminal justice.

The first few chapters summarize much of the past research on crowding and our previous published results on prison crowding. The subsequent chapters focus on recently completed analyses of our extensive data sets. One chapter focuses on the influence of gender and race on a person's adjustment to crowded conditions, while another deals with the degree to which various background factors influence reactivity to crowded settings. One chapter evaluates the health-related findings of our studies. The last two chapters deal with the theoretical and practical implications of our work.

This book was not intended to be the final word on the topic of prison crowding. Many important questions remain, and the difficulty, danger, and expense of the research will limit progress on this topic. Yet, much has been accomplished since our tentative beginnings fifteen years ago. It is hoped that future research efforts will be able to build on the foundation laid by our work and that of others.

2
Effects of Crowding in General

Concern with the effects of overcrowding has been expressed for many years. Malthus warned about the danger of overpopulation in terms of natural resources in the 1800s. Benjamin Franklin once stated: "There is in short no bound to the prolific nature of plants or animals but what is made by their crowding and interfering with each other's means of subsistence" (Franklin, 1969). Today we are expressing similar concerns (Russell, 1984). Starvation, water shortages, pollution, and "eternal" traffic jams are just a few of the obvious symptoms of population pressures in our world. Social scientists have warned about the dangers of overcrowding (Calhoun, 1970; Ehrlich & Ehrlich, 1970; Zlutnick & Altman, 1972). Crowding has been blamed for a variety of social ills such as deteriorating quality of life in cities, crime, and the breakdown of families (Zlutnick & Altman, 1972). These concerns were further stimulated by Calhoun's (1962) widely publicized studies with rodents showing a variety of deleterious effects of crowding.

Although the commonly held conceptions about crowding may seem reasonable to most laypersons, social scientists have taken a variety of approaches to determine whether these are warranted. For a number of years, those with a sociological bent have examined the influence of density in cities and countries by means of archival studies. Typically, the density of housing and the surrounding neighborhood was related to various measures of pathology such as delinquency, violence, mental health, and mortality. Other scientists studied the impact of crowding on animals in both field and laboratory settings. In the 1970s, laboratory studies of density with humans became popular. More recently, efforts have been directed at assessing human reactions to density in controlled field studies in settings such as college dormitories and prisons. Each of these approaches has its limitations, but they all have been a source of useful information. We will briefly summarize the major findings of the four different areas of study to provide a context for the research on prison crowding.

In discussing the impact of crowding, a major problem one encounters is the variety of ways in which this concept has been defined. Some studies employ measures of density that focus on the primary living environment (internal density) such as the number of people per room. Other studies focus on density outside the primary living environment (external density) such as the number of apartments per unit and housing units per acre. Another important distinction is based on whether the density variation is primarily spatial or social. An environment could vary in spaciousness while maintaining a constant number of inhabitants (spatial density), or it could vary in the number of inhabitants but not in the amount of space available for each inhabitant (social density). Another common distinction is made between density as a physical condition and crowding as the subjective experience of density-related discomfort (Stokols, 1972). The term overcrowding is also often used in reference to density problems, but the reference point for this term seems to be the capacity of a setting. If the number of individuals exceeds capacity, it is deemed to be overcrowded. However, neither of these terms are very useful from a scientific standpoint in that they do not clearly specify those conditions under which deleterious effects will occur. A setting may exceed capacity and not evidence density-related effects, while such effects might be observed in environments that are below capacity. Stokols (1972) suggested that the term density be used to describe objective conditions of spatial constriction. The term crowding was to be reserved for those conditions in which an individual experienced limitations of space. We presumed that not all forms of density would have similar effects and that a variety of personal and situational factors would influence the impact of density. These assumptions have been amply supported by the subsequent literature and the data reported here. In this book, the term crowding will be used generically to refer to a wide variety of conditions of physical and social density because of its common usage, without the assumption that these conditions inevitably produce pathology.

Crowding Studies with Animals

Some of the most dramatic findings on crowding have come from animal studies. One frequently cited study by Christian (1963) examined deer on an island that suffered a high mortality rate after experiencing increased density levels. Autopsies revealed enlarged adrenal glands, one common result of stress (Selye, 1956). Calhoun's studies with rodents revealed similar evidence of stress-related effects of overcrowding. In one of his early studies, he noted that rodents stabilize their population at much lower levels than are supportable by the environment (Calhoun, 1962). In a later study, he found that a mouse colony that was allowed unlimited growth and adequate resources declined in population after reaching a level of 2,200 in an area designed for 6,000 or more. The deterioration of maternal behavior and the high rates of infant mortality led to complete extinction of the colony (Calhoun, 1973).

Similar results have been observed in Calhoun's (1962) experimental laboratory studies. Eighty rats were housed in four connected enclosures in a 10 by 14 ft room. The population was kept at 80 by removing infants who survived weaning. Because of the design of access among the pens, most of the rat population was concentrated in two central pens. The end pens were dominated by a dominant male and his "harem" of females. While those rats in the end pens remained healthy and normal in behavior, those in the central pens began to exhibit various forms of pathology. Males exhibited disturbances in sexual behavior (e.g., hypersexuality), aggressive behavior, withdrawal, and cannibalism. Females' reproductive capacity and maternal behavior deteriorated, which led to low birth survival rates. Calhoun (1962) attributed these various effects to the strain of having to deal with large numbers of rats in a confined space.

The studies by Christian and Calhoun are the best known, but many other studies have found similar evidence of crowding-induced pathology. Susceptibility to infection (Brayton & Brain, 1974), organ damage (Myers, Hale, Mykytowycz, & Hughes, 1971), and increased blood pressure (Henry, Stephens, Axelrod, & Mueller, 1971) have been observed under conditions of high density.

Although the animal studies are quite consistent in showing stress-related effects of high levels of density, many have questioned the relevance of these results for humans. Certainly these findings provide a baseline by which to judge human data, and they may be a basis for furthering theoretical development. However, it is often argued that the unique adaptive capacities of humans make them immune from many of the dramatic effects observed in animal studies (Freedman, 1979). Obviously, this is an empirical question which has been the subject of a large number of studies.

Correlational Studies with Humans

It is often presumed that crowded cities present their residents with many annoyances not associated with less crowded areas. Crowded cities may be characterized by a high density of people in the streets and neighborhoods, noise, traffic jams, pollution, and crime as well as limited space in dwelling units. Sociological studies have attempted to tap these features indirectly in various density measures such as people per census tract, people per acre, people per building, buildings per acre, and individuals per unit. It was presumed that these measures would tap the degree of crowding-related strain experienced by residents and these in turn would be associated with increased levels of pathology such as hospital admission, mortality, and juvenile delinquency. Although some studies failed to take into account differences in income and socioeconomic levels, for the past 20 years most of the studies have attempted to control for such factors statistically.

A number of the sociological studies have found evidence for a density-pathology relationship for city residents. Schmitt (1966) found relationships between density and death rate, tuberculosis, mental hospital admissions, and juvenile delinquency in Honolulu. Booth and Welch (1973) found density to be related to a variety of different crimes in data from 65 countries. Galle and co-workers (1972) reported relationships between density and mortality, fertility, mental hospital admissions, and juvenile delinquency in Chicago. A study in the Netherlands found evidence for density-related health problems such as mortality and heart disease (Levy & Herzog, 1974), while a study in Germany reported a relationship between density and mortality (Manton & Myers, 1977).

The results of these studies seem to provide strong evidence that urban density may have a variety of negative effects. However, there are a number of studies with results that do not support such a strong conclusion. A study by Winsborough (1965) in Chicago found high levels of density to be related to low levels of mortality, tuberculosis, and public assistance. Freedman and colleagues (1975) found density to be related only to mental hospital terminations. Studies by Levy and Herzog (1974), Cholden and Roneck (1975), and Mitchell (1971) provide similar evidence of either no relationship between density and negative effects, or even positive effects. Some studies have found living alone to be related to increases in usage of stress-reducing drugs, suicides, and admissions to mental hospitals (Galle et al., 1972; Levy & Herzog, 1974; Collette & Webb, 1975).

Thus the evidence for a density-pathology relationship in urban settings is rather mixed. Furthermore, there are a number of problems inherent in the correlational approach employed in these studies (cf. Fischer, Baldassare, & Ofshe, 1975), not the least of which is the uncertainty as to the causal nature of the relationships observed. Even when all of the obvious socioeconomic factors are controlled statistically, many other factors could account for the differences between low and high density areas. Individuals who gravitate toward dense urban areas may have physical or mental health problems, antisocial tendencies, or they may be forced to live there by economic or social pressures. Noise and pollution in crowded areas may account for effects attributed to density, and high crime rates in high density areas may be a significant source of stress in itself. Finally, the various density measures employed may not accurately reflect the degree of crowding experienced by residents. Familiarity with residents, traffic flow, and the arrangement of both internal and external space are likely to influence the experiences.

Given these problems with the approach and the inconsistency of the results, it is not surprising that researchers have increasingly turned to other approaches such as experiments and field studies.

Experimental Studies with Humans

Experimental studies have been confined mostly to brief laboratory exposures to varying density levels. Most sessions were less than 1 hour, and density was varied by having subjects perform tasks or interact in groups and/or rooms of varying sizes. These studies were designed to assess the impact of short-term crowding on emotional responses, task performance, and social inclinations (e.g., degree of cooperation or hostility). These studies are commendable because of their precision and control, but the applicability of the findings to chronic conditions of crowding may be limited.

A few studies have observed increased physiological responses under high density conditions such as skin conductance (Aiello, Epstein, & Karlin, 1975), palmar sweating (Saegert, 1974), blood pressure, and heart rate (Evans, 1979). High density levels have also been associated with impaired task performance, especially on complex tasks (e.g., Aiello et al., 1975; Paulus, Annis, Seta, Schkade, & Matthews, 1976; Saegert, 1974). Although some studies have failed to find such effects (e.g., Freedman, Klevansky, & Ehrlich, 1971), it appears that the features of the task setting, such as the degree of perceived control and the use of multiple tasks, determine whether effects are observed (Paulus & Matthews, 1980).

Some studies have examined emotional and social reactions to being crowded. In general, it appears that increases in social density usually produce negative reactions and a tendency toward social withdrawal in the form of increased social distance and reduced eye contact (Baum & Koman, 1976). Reactions to spatial density appear to be sex-specific, with males reacting negatively and withdrawing under conditions of high spatial density, and females reacting positively and demonstrating increased sociability (Freedman, Levy, Buchanan, & Price, 1972; Ross, Layton, Erickson, & Schopler, 1973). These results have been interpreted as reflecting either different coping styles of males and females or their differential sensitivity to personal space (Paulus, 1980).

A few studies have examined the effects of crowding on aggressive tendencies in the laboratory. Some studies suggest that aggressive tendencies are dependent on the sexual composition of the group. Freedman and associates (1972) demonstrated that males respond more competitively in a game in small rooms than in large ones, whereas the reverse is true for females. Females in a low density jury situation gave harsher sentences than those in a higher density situation. Stokols, Rall, Pinner, and Schopler (1973) found that males, but not females, perceive themselves as more aggressive in small rooms compared with large ones. Baum and Koman (1976) found that men exhibited aggressive posturing (in terms of seating position and interaction style) when anticipating being crowded in a small room. This evidence indicates that only males may react aggressively to spatially crowded conditions. Furthermore, other studies suggest that even with males, high levels of density may actually reduce the tendency to aggress (Matthews, Paulus, & Baron, 1979). These results suggest that moderate levels of spatial density may, among males, instigate aggressive tendencies designed to reduce the spatial proximity of others. However, at very high levels of density, this strategy may not be seen as effective and may be replaced by a tendency to withdraw.

The laboratory research has thus demonstrated a variety of effects of short-term crowding. However, the effects seem to depend on a complex array of variables such as spatial versus social density, levels of density, and sexual composition of the group. The primary utility of these studies has been in aiding the development of theoretical notions such as arousal, interference, control, and density-intensity. These will be discussed in Chapter 8.

One reason for the rather tenuous relationships observed in the laboratory situation utilizing humans may be that the laboratory setting is temporary and elective and may not engage various emotional and psychological processes. This problem is reduced in field studies that examine the influence of density in real-world situations.

Field Studies

Field studies of crowding have been done in a wide variety of settings ranging from college dormitories to naval ships. Interestingly, one of the first situations studied was the school playground. These studies focused primarily on the occurrence of aggressive behavior. Hutt and Vaizey (1966) reported increased aggression and reduced cooperation with increased density in a playground. Subsequent studies have shown that such effects may occur only when resources on the playground are restricted (Rohe & Patterson, 1974), and that very high levels of density may induce withdrawal rather than aggression (Loo, 1972, 1978). This finding is in accord with that of the laboratory studies.

One of the most popular sites for field studies of crowding has been the college dormitory because of obvious ease of access. A number of investigators have examined the effect of adding an extra person to a double room. Baron and co-workers (1976) and Aiello and associates (1975) found that this change led to negative emotional reactions, increased physiological stress, and some indications of poorer health. Another series of studies on dormitory crowding was done by Baum and Valins (1977). This research compared long corridor dorms containing 17 to 22 double-occupancy rooms with short corridor dorms containing 10 double-occupancy rooms and dorms containing small four-to-six-person suites with self-contained bath and lounge facilities. Relative to the other two dormitory types, residents of long corridor dorms felt crowded and demonstrated withdrawal and isolation behavior both in and outside the dorms. The reactions tended to stay at a similar level or increase through the period of residence, suggesting a lack of adaptation to the crowding experienced. Baum and Valins interpret their results as being due to the uncontrollable and unwanted interactions with strangers to which long corridor residents were exposed.

One of the issues addressed by the sociological studies discussed earlier was that of household crowding. These studies found some evidence of a crowding-pathology relationship, but were beset by interpretational problems. Some field studies of household density have, however, also found that housing density can lead to negative effects. One study employed comprehensive physical examinations and found modest relationships between household density and a variety of health problems (Booth & Cowell, 1976). Gove, Hughes, and Galle (1979) obtained similar results in Chicago. Some other studies did not obtain results that were equally strong (for review, see Cox, Paulus, McCain, & Karlovac, 1982).

Several studies of household crowding have obtained a variety of nonhealth-related effects. Rodin (1976) found evidence of density-induced passivity or helplessness. She found that the greater the number of people in a three-room apartment, the less likely the children from these apartments would utilize the option to exercise their own choices. Junior high school students living in dense home environments exhibited inferior performance on problem-solving tasks. A study by Saegert (1982) focused on the effects of residential density on low income children. High density conditions involved living with a large number of individuals in an apartment in a large building. These children evidenced a variety of behavior problems, anxiety, and hyperactive distractibility. They also exhibited lower reading comprehension and vocabulary scores than those living in low density housing.

The field studies cited have provided generally consistent evidence that density in a variety of real-world settings can have deleterious effects. Similar results have been obtained on naval ships (Dean, Pugh, & Gunderson, 1975, 1978) and in prisons (Cox, Paulus, & McCain, 1984; D'Atri, Fitzgerald, Kasl, & Ostfeld, 1981; Paulus, McCain, & Cox, 1985).

This brief overview suggests that crowding can be a source of problems for both animals and humans in short-term laboratory and long-term real-world situations, in urban environments, and in residential housing. The observed effects have ranged from negative affect and impaired task performance to disruption of social behavior and deterioration of health. These patterns of results certainly provide a solid basis for expecting strong effects due to prison crowding. The prison inmates often encounter conditions that are much more crowded than any conditions they encounter in their free-world life. In the next two chapters, we will examine the published research on this question.

3
Prison Crowding Research

Although prison crowding has been a major concern of corrections and government officials, surprisingly few studies on the actual impact of crowding exist. This undoubtedly reflects the relative inaccessibility of the prison as a research site and the difficulties of conducting research in a prison environment. Research on crowding that is likely to yield results that might be unfavorable and politically troublesome is particularly difficult to accomplish.

It appears that the major underlying concern of the judiciary is that crowded prison conditions represent cruel and unusual punishment (e.g., *Rhodes v. Chapman*, 1981). Given the expense of prison construction, it would seem important to know as much as possible about the psychological and physical impact of various prison housing conditions. Although billions of dollars have been spent on prison construction in the past 15 years, total funding for research on the effects of prison crowding has probably not reached $1 million. As a result, research in this area can only be considered as being in the "infant state." We have developed a broad picture, but precise and definitive information about many important issues is lacking. In this chapter, we will summarize and evaluate briefly all of the published studies done by other scholars.

Research studies of crowding tend to fall into three different categories. Some have focused on the impact of overall prison crowding on the general prison population. Others have directly examined inmates living in different housing conditions on various psychological and physiological measures. A third group has examined the impact of changes in housing conditions.

Archival Studies of Overall Prison Crowding

Many studies of overall prison crowding have relied on data obtained from prison records. These studies are especially valuable in illuminating the relationship of crowding to low-frequency events such as suicides, deaths,

---

This chapter was written in collaboration with Verne Cox.

and violence where large data bases are required for analysis. These studies have been concerned with several interrelated issues. Some are concerned with the influence of institution size, and have tried to determine whether large prisons that hold many inmates in the same institution have a negative impact on health, prison behavior, and recidivism. Others have examined the impact of degree of institutional crowding relative to some baseline, either a past level of crowding or the design capacity of the institution. Although these studies may be informative about the issue of overall prison crowding, they have a number of drawbacks. Prison archival records are often inaccurate, and great care has to be taken to cross-validate information obtained from the records. Measures of prison size or the degree of overcrowding relative to capacity typically ignore specific types of housing within a prison. For example, a prison can be rated as over capacity if single cells are converted to double occupancy. A similar over-capacity value might be obtained in another prison where being over capacity reflected an increase in number of inmates housed in dormitory space relative to the number of inmates in single or double cells. Some prisons would be rated as within designed capacity even though a substantial number of inmates are housed in dormitories. Such prisons may yield more negative effects compared with institutions with single or double cells that are over capacity, even though the space per inmate for the institution with dormitory housing as a whole meets a designed capacity criterion. Another problem with some archival studies is the combining of data from multiple institutions. This procedure ignores unique characteristics that might result in greater crowding-related effects in some institutions compared with others with the same capacity rating. For example, in most prisons, single- and double-cell housing is preferred, but in one study (D'Atri & Ostfeld, 1975), dormitory housing was preferred in spite of the fact that higher levels of stress were observed in the dormitory housing.

Most of the archival studies have focused on the relationship of crowding to measures of social misconduct, including assaultive behavior directed towards inmates or staff. It is typically assumed that crowding might be related to increased disruptive or assaultive behavior. Such a prediction could be derived from the notion that crowding increases frustration, irritability, or the opportunity for aggression-evoking encounters which, in turn, may be related to increased violence or misconduct (Zillman, 1979). However, it has also been shown that although moderate levels of irritability may increase aggression, very high levels of irritability may be related to reduced aggression (Baron, 1977). At very high levels of irritability, individuals may focus primarily on ways to reduce their unpleasant state, rather than get involved in hostile encounters.

The first published study of the impact of prison crowding on social misconduct was a small-scale study by Megargee (1977). He obtained disciplinary infraction data from inmates who were housed in dormitory housing that was less spacious than usual during the renovation of several housing units. During the 3-year period of the study, space per person ranged from 55 to 77 sq ft. The dormitory housing provided a privacy screen around each bunk. Megargee found that there was a strong positive relationship between spatial density and the rate of disciplinary infractions, but that population level was not related to the rate of disciplinary infractions. Jan (1980) obtained generally similar results. It may be that disciplinary infraction rates that include aggressive encounters are especially exacerbated by spatial density, since physical proximity would facilitate confrontations. Megargee also examined the influence of ambient temperature on disruptive behavior. Contrary to common intuition, temperature, even in the uncomfortable range of 85°F or higher, was not associated with higher rates of disciplinary infractions.

In a much more extensive study, Nacci, Teitelbaum, and Prather (1977) examined the relationship between inmate violence and a measure of population density defined in terms of federal standards for living space per inmate, relative to the actual space per inmate in a particular institution. They obtained information on total assaults, assaults on inmates, and total disciplinary infractions. The data were obtained from 37 federal correctional institutions for a 3-year period from 1973 to 1976. These investigators reported statistically reliable correlations between density and rates of total assaults and assaults on inmates. The strongest relationship between violence and crowding was obtained in less crowded institutions housing younger inmates. However, the age–violence relationship was not found in more crowded institutions housing both young and older inmates. The fact that there was a negative correlation between density and violence in more crowded intermediate institutions strengthens the contention that crowding is not necessarily positively related to violent behavior and that more intense crowding may be associated with lessened violent behavior when compared to less crowded environs. Nacci and co-workers (1977) attribute the negative relationship between violence and crowding in the more crowded institutions to social withdrawal and more social cohesiveness among inmates as crowding intensifies. Thus, the relationship between crowding and violence is not a simple one, and the degree of crowding and age range of the inmate population can be determining factors (see also Ellis, 1984). The measure of population density employed by Nacci and co-workers is relatively imprecise since it does not distinguish between types of housing (e.g., cells versus dorms). On the basis of our own research and the findings reported by Gaes and McGuire (1985), one would expect that inmates housed in dormitory conditions may have contributed disproportionately to the relationship between assaults and density when a positive correlation is obtained.

Gaes and McGuire (1985) examined the relationship between measures of prison violence and crowding for 19 federal prisons over a 33-month period. As in that 1977 study, the crowding measure related total institution living space to the number of inmates and failed to distinguish between various types of housing. A supporting analysis suggested that the proportion of inmates in dormitory housing was as reliable a correlate of inmate violence as an overall capacity index. The Gaes and McGuire analysis indicated that the strongest predictor of prison inmate violent behavior was the crowding index, whereas other variables such as inmate age, staff-inmate ratio, institution size, and inmate transfers were not strongly related to indices of inmate violence. It should be noted that federal prisons, even when over capacity, have predominantly nonviolent populations in relatively benign conditions as compared with most state prisons.

Ruback and Carr (1984) examined disciplinary infraction rates in a prison with female inmates and found that prison population level was significantly correlated with disciplinary infraction rates. The findings were based on archival records for 561 female inmates who had served at least 6 months in prison. The prison population ranged from 269 to 399 during the period 1971–1979. As in the study of Nacci and co-workers (1977), age was also significantly correlated with misconduct. Thus females appear to respond to crowding with higher rates of misconduct as it had been found with males in other studies.

Farrington and Nuttall (1980) examined the relationship of crowding to disciplinary infractions and recidivism in England. The prisons provided cells designed for one occupant, and being over capacity involved housing from two to three inmates in some portion of the single-occupant housing. They found that degree of overcrowding was positively correlated with recidivism (the difference between predicted and actual reconviction rates). They also examined the influence of the size of the institution and found that this variable did not relate significantly to recidivism, but that smaller prisons tended to have higher offense rates. However, Farrington and Nuttall indicated that there were considerable differences in inmate population characteristics of the various prisons studied, which might account for the latter finding.

Another way to study the impact of institution crowding is to determine whether changes in population within the same unit are related to changes in disruptive behavior. Bruehl, Horvat, and George (1979) reported interesting findings for a chemical abuse subunit of the Federal Correctional Institution at Terminal Island, California. The population of the subunit increased substantially (33%) from a stable 7-month baseline population. The housing consisted of cells designed for one occupant. During the period of increase in unit population, some of the single cells housed two inmates. Consequently, change in social density constituted housing two inmates in some of the single-occupant cells. Social and spatial density changes were totally confounded. Increased population was related to increases in the percentage of escapes, disciplinary reports, and commitments to administrative detention. No changes were observed on these variables elsewhere in the prison where population level was unchanged during the period of the study. Although the results of this study are generally consistent with other research reported in this volume, it should be noted that this study had a relatively small sample and was limited to the examination of one unit.

In a study of prisons in Canada, Porporino and Dudley (1984) employed an excess capacity index similar to those employed by Gaes and McGuire (1985) and Nacci and co-workers (1977). However, the only variation in housing was between single cells that contained one or two occupants. Consequently, the capacity index and measure of crowding can be seen as being related to the proportion of an institution's housing that consists of doubled-bunked single cells. Porporino and Dudley found that when inmate turnover or flow was accounted for, the index of crowding was negatively correlated with violent behavior. However, it should be noted that turnover may have been particularly salient in this study because the study did not include dormitory housing. In our own research, we have found a number of instances where our measures of crowding effects failed to discriminate between cells with one or two occupants.

Ekland-Olson (1986) recently examined the relationship between prison crowding and violence in the Texas prison system before and after the changes prompted by the *Ruiz v. Estelle* (1980) decision. Ekland-Olson argues that there is no relationship between crowding and measures of violence such as homicides and inmate assaults on inmates or staff. Ekland-Olson's definition of crowding is space per person as reflected in a designed capacity criterion. Ekland-Olson found that homicides actually declined in the presence of increasing prison population in the pre-Ruiz period, and subsequently increased dramatically during the period when the social structure of the prison system was disrupted by court-ordered changes. During the period when Ekland-Olson reported no relationship between crowding and prison violence, the Texas prison system was undergoing chaotic changes in inmate social organization. This was due to the elimination of the building tender system, which provided certain inmates with considerable control over other inmates. However, Ekland-Olson also indicated that recordkeeping may have improved in the post-Ruiz period, and it is during this period that there is a strong relationship between system population level and homicides. Other measures of violence during the period 1979–1984, such as inmate assaults, were systematically related to prison population levels with the exception of the year 1980.

Ellis (1984) reviewed the studies regarding crowding and prison violence and argued that most existing studies fail to recognize that alterations in staff responses and reporting of violence occur with variations in social density. He argues that in contrast to some reports, such as that of Gaes and McGuire (1985), age is a major factor in prison violence associated with high social density. In addition, Ellis also attributes violence commonly associated with crowding to changes in the rate of movements of inmates within the prison and the change in rate of flow of inmates into and out of an institution during increases in social density.

Direct Assessments of Inmates in Different Types of Housing

Some studies have examined inmates directly to determine the impact of living in specific housing conditions. These studies circumvent the problems inherent in the archival studies, but they are not without problems of their own. Care must be taken to ensure that inmates from particular housing types do not differ in important ways such as security level, time in prison, etc. The majority of studies have focused on a very limited number of variables and housing types. Other institution variables can influence these measures, including institution size and rate of turnover of the institution population.

A study by D'Atri and Ostfeld (1975) examined the relationship between a physiological correlate of stress, blood pressure, and housing density. They reported that blood pressure values were systematically related to type of housing in three different prisons. Dormitory housing yielded higher values compared with values obtained for single- or double-cell housing. Social density appears to be the primary determinant of the results, since in some cases dormitories provided as much space per person as single cells, and double cells provided less space per person than dormitories. Unlike most prisons, inmates in the three prisons preferred dormitory housing. In spite of this preference, the dormitory housing yielded stronger indications of stress as reflected in elevated blood pressure values. They also found that inmates with the shortest and longest history of confinement in the prisons had higher blood pressure values than inmates with intermediate confinement histories. A major limitation of this study is the small number of measures employed. Only blood pressure measurements, questions about attitudes toward guards, and the prisoners' perceived spaciousness of the environment were used.

Ruback and co-workers (Ruback & Carr, 1984; Ruback, Carr, & Hopper, 1986) focused on the role of perceived control in mediating observed crowding effects. A substantial amount of literature in the stress domain suggests that this factor may be important in determining the extent to which stress has negative consequences for health (Cohen, Glass, & Phillips, 1979). Ruback and co-workers (1986) examined perceived control and its relationship to other measures obtained via a questionnaire answered by inmates living in dormitories which housed 8 to 50 inmates. However, no attempt was made to distinguish between social and spatial density. Inmates housed in 50-occupant dormitories with 35 sq ft per person were grouped for analysis with inmates living in 20-person trailers with 72 sq ft per person, inmates in an 18-occupant dormitory with 38 sq ft per person, and inmates in an 8-occupant dormitory with 36 sq ft per person. They reported that perceived control was significantly correlated with measures (obtained from questionnaires) of stress, room evaluation, and physical symptoms suggestive of impaired health. Because the findings were correlative, no conclusions can be drawn regarding the causal role of perceived control.

In another study, Ruback and Carr (1984) examined crowding in a women's prison. This study represents one of the very few that involved female inmates. As these investigators noted, laboratory studies have identified sex differences in response to crowding, and it is important to determine whether such differences are observable under the more severe and naturalistic conditions found in prisons. The housing consisted of single rooms and double rooms that provided 76 sq ft of space, large rooms that housed four inmates and provided 160 sq ft of space, and trailers that housed 20 inmates and provided 780 sq ft of space. Via questionnaires, these investigators examined the relationship of crowding to illness complaints, perception of the physical environment, perceived stress, and perceived control. Housing with larger numbers of inmates was rated more negatively, but no other effects of housing were observed. However, greater perceived control was correlated with more positive ratings of the housing and fewer reports of physical health symptoms. The findings of the role of perceived control in reactions to housing and physical health are consistent with prior research (Cohen et al., 1979). However, since they failed to find differences in perceived control and health among the different housing types, the implications of this study for the crowding issue are not clear. It is possible that the specific architectural features of the more dense housing limited the impact of the social density factor.

Effects of Changes in Housing

Although studies comparing individuals living in different housing units can provide much useful information, one major drawback to these studies is that inmates are not randomly assigned to their housing units. For example, less crowded housing may be assigned based on seniority or good behavior. Alternatively, housing assignment may be determined by program or job assignments. Sometimes one can deal with these problems in the design of one's study or by statistical techniques, but the best alternative is to examine the same inmates as they move from one housing unit to another. It is particularly important to observe the influence of moving to more crowded and less crowded housing. This has been accomplished in two studies.

A study by D'Atri and colleagues (1981) examined inmates as they were transferred from a single cell to dorms or from dorms to singles. The dorms were large open rooms with 20 to 30 beds. Those transferred from cells to dorms had increases in systolic (but not diastolic) blood pressure. Those who moved from one cell to another or remained in cells did not evidence significant changes in blood pressure. A small number of inmates who were transferred from dorms back to cells showed a nonsignificant decrease in blood pressure. Even though housing type was related to differences in age, length of confinement, and body bulk, effects remained the same when these variables were controlled statistically. Factors such as race, education, and recidivism were also controlled.

Wener and Keys (1986) examined two identical prison housing units in which the population density simultaneously increased in one and decreased in the other. The common administrative milieu and physical layout of the units provided an unusual degree of control over these variables. The two identical units were designed to house 48 inmates in single cells. One unit actually housed an average of 64 inmates with the addition of a second bunk in single rooms. The other unit was initially held to 48 inmates in single cells. Subsequently, the units were equalized in population by removing the second bunks from single cells and providing cots in hallways. So one unit experienced a decline in overall population and the other an increase. Following these changes, both units held approximately similar numbers of inmates (56 inmates). Probably because of the unusual opportunity for control of physical and administrative variables, these investigators were able to detect changes in a variety of variables sensitive to crowding, even though the changes in population were modest and the actual degree of crowding was relatively modest as compared with that often observed in prison settings. Sick call rates and perceived crowding scores were higher in the more populous unit prior to equalization of the units, and interestingly were higher in the unit that experienced an increase in population following the equalization of inmate populations in the two units. This "contrast" effect is reminiscent of informal observations we made of inmate reactions to a change to double-cell housing from single-cell housing at Pontiac Correctional Center in Illinois in 1978. These inmates appeared to be quite disturbed by the prospect of double-cell housing. Not long after the change at Pontiac, riots erupted that destroyed many of the housing units of the prison. Inmates may be particularly sensitive to increases in the degree of crowding relative to past standards or levels.

The housing change studies have provided strong support for the conclusions drawn from the archival and housing-type studies. Their greatest contribution is in providing clear evidence of crowding effects independent of other related variables.

Summary and Evaluation

The studies reviewed provide rather consistent evidence of a relationship between crowding and disciplinary infractions and illness complaints. However, a major drawback of the set of studies reviewed is their limited

scope. The archival studies have examined only a small set of prison systems and have focused mostly on disruptive behavior. Only one of the
studies examined institution size, and only one evaluated the impact of
change in population. Our research team obtained archival data on a broad
variety of health-related measures from a large number of systems. This
allowed for an examination of the effects of size of institution, degree of
overcrowding, and changes in population (see Chapter 5).

   The studies in individual units typically used only a small number of
measures or compared only a few housing types. Some studies were able to
analyze separately the impact of social and spatial density, whereas the
majority of studies have examined environments where these two variables
are confounded. It is difficult from these studies to make a specific deter-
mination about the influence of the various components of crowding
(space, number, or privacy). The studies in our research program were
designed to provide information on the impact of these different components on a broad range of psychological and physiological measures in a
wide variety of prisons (see Chapters 4 and 5).

   Research on prison crowding has also been somewhat confusing as to the
role of personal, social, and environmental factors in reactions to different
types of prison conditions. For example, there is some controversy about
the role of age in the crowding-violence relationship (Ellis, 1984). Some of
the research suggests that inmate turnover or population flow can account
for effects typically attributed to crowding. While privacy and perceived
control have been viewed as important variables accounting for crowding
effects, evidence in support of this contention is not abundant. A major
goal of the research to be presented was to develop an understanding of
the variables that influence reactions to crowded housing and of those
processes that underlie the effects of crowding in prisons and other environments (Chapters 6–8).

4
Prison Housing

The remainder of this book will focus on the major results of the research program on crowding in prisons done by the team from the University of Texas at Arlington. In Chapter 1, the process of searching for feasible prison sites and some of the details of our research trips were described. This chapter will deal primarily with the results of the studies on the effects of prison housing. The early studies will be reviewed briefly, and the detailed results of a major project stimulated by the early studies will be presented.

Early Studies

Initially, our major energies were invested in visiting prisons all over the United States to find suitable research sites. One of the first prisons visited was Texarkana Federal Correctional Institution (FCI) in Texarkana, Texas. We immediately recognized its potential as a research site. It had a wide range of housing—singles, doubles, and dormitories. Furthermore, the singles and doubles were located in hallways or units that varied in the number of rooms, anywhere from 10 to 32. Dormitories included large dorms housing up to 48 men in double bunks, similar-sized dorms housing 20 men with single bunks, and a dorm housing up to 50 men that was architecturally divided into smaller sections of about 10 to 20 men each. On our first visit, we employed questionnaires and a tolerance-for-crowding task. In later visits, we added a palmar sweat measure and a motor-coordination task.

At about the same time, we visited Dallas County Jail and discovered a broad range of housing conditions that presented a wide variety of social and spatial density conditions. We were excited by our discovery that prisons and jails were feasible sites for examining a number of questions about crowding. These observations, coupled with the success of our first few visits to Texarkana, prompted us to publish a brief report to educate others on the potential utility of prison and jail studies of crowding (Paulus, McCain, & Cox, 1973).

Our first detailed publication of results did not occur until we were confident of the consistency and stability of our results. This required a 2-year
effort of three visits to Texarkana FCI (Paulus, Cox, McCain, & Chandler,
1975). Our concerns in this study were twofold. First, we wanted to determine the relative importance of space and number of residents in prison
housing. Although prison legal suits had focused on space, it seemed possible that the number of residents sharing a common space might be equally, if not more, important. We primarily examined inmates in singles and
dormitories (26 to 44 inmates), with space per person ranging from 31 to
84 sq ft. To our surprise, we found that spatial density did not influence
ratings of the environment, but social density did have an effect (Paulus
et al., 1975). This was the first indication that contrary to the common
perspective of the day, the number of residents with which one has to
share one's living unit may be more important than the amount of space
available.

We obtained several other interesting results. We had anticipated that
living under crowded conditions would lead to an increased tolerance of
crowding simply as a result of adaptation. However, we found for two of
the visits that those living in dormitories were less tolerant of crowding
using a simulation task. This task required inmates to place as many small
figures in a simulated dorm as they could without overcrowding it. Furthermore, those inmates who had lived in the dorms the longest demonstrated less tolerance than other dorm residents. We interpreted these results as indicating that those exposed to high levels of social density and
low levels of privacy will increase their valuation of privacy and low levels
of social density. These results were contrary to expectations based on a
simple adaptation perspective.

While we were conducting this series of studies, we became convinced
that when crowding in prisons and jails reached high enough levels, inmates might in fact be experiencing a significant level of stress and a related
deterioration of health. To assess this possibility, health records were
obtained both at Texarkana FCI and Dallas County Jail (McCain, Cox, &
Paulus, 1976). At Texarkana FCI, the frequency and nature of visits were
obtained from medical records of 247 inmates, some of whom also partici-
pated in the study cited previously. Data were obtained for up to a 6-month
period. An illness rate was obtained by dividing the number of days in the
last housing unit into the number of visits to the clinic. Only those who had
lived at least 30 days in their current housing condition were included in
our analyses. This was done to allow a sufficient period of time for the
housing unit to influence the inmate's health status. At the county jail, we
were limited to obtaining written requests for medical attention submitted
by inmates. These were obtained for all of the inmates for a period of 5
weeks.

At Texarkana FCI, inmates in dormitories experienced higher illness
complaint rates than single cell inmates (.033 versus .015 daily rate). In the
county jail, inmates who lived in units that were high in both social and

spatial density submitted more requests for medical attention for 4 of the 5 weeks than did the inmates living in less dense quarters. We interpreted these results as reflecting the impact of stress experienced in crowded living conditions.

We were cognizant of the interpretational problems of the illness complaint measure (cf. Mechanic, 1976). It provides an important but indirect indication of the inmate's health status. Clinic visits can also be interpreted to reflect nonhealth-related factors such as desire for attention or medication. Early in our research program, we decided to obtain additional physiological indicators of the reactions of inmates to housing.

In one study of Texarkana FCI, we employed a measure of palmar sweating that had been used in a variety of situations to assess stress reactions (Dabbs, Johnson, & Leventhal, 1968). This technique involves obtaining a print from one finger with a special solution. The dried print is used to obtain a count of the number of pores open in a 1-cm^2 central area. The more pores that are open, the greater is the presumed physiological autonomic reactivity to one's environment. Inmates in a wide variety of housing were assessed, and it was found that palmar sweating increased with increased social density, but was unrelated to spatial density (Cox, Paulus, McCain, & Schkade, 1979). These findings were consistent with our earlier findings. Subsequently, we had an opportunity to examine feelings of crowding and blood pressures of inmates who were housed in cells with one, two, or five other inmates in a large state prison. The two-man cells had 29 sq ft per person, while the three- and six-man cells had 19 sq ft per person (Fig. 4–1). The inmates in the three- and six-man cells exhibited

FIGURE 4–1. Cell housing three men in a 58 sq ft cell in a state prison.

higher feelings of crowding and elevated blood pressures relative to double-cell inmates (Paulus, McCain, & Cox, 1978).

Thus toward the end of the 1970s, we had accumulated a consistent body of evidence from a variety of prisons and jails. Yet, most of our data had come from one institution (Texarkana FCI), and these data and the data from other prisons were limited in scope. We decided that a comprehensive analysis of a variety of different prisons and housing types was required to determine the generality of our earlier findings and to document more precisely the factors influencing inmate reactions to housing. The U.S. Department of Justice agreed and provided generous support for an exciting but exhausting 2-year program to accomplish these aims.

Research Procedures

The data that will be discussed here was gathered during a 2-year period from 1,240 inmates in six federal prisons (cf. McCain, Cox, & Paulus, 1980). In each prison, we randomly selected a sample from various housing units that varied in degree of crowding (e.g., singles, doubles, and open dorms). These inmates were asked to report to a testing station in groups of six every 15 minutes. When they arrived, the study was explained and informed consent forms were given to the volunteers. Typically, 90% or more of the inmates agreed to participate. In most cases, no incentives were offered, although on some occasions we offered a soft drink for participation.

At the research station, inmates first had their blood pressure taken, using an automated electrosphygmomanometer, and were asked to rate how crowded they felt in their current housing on a 4-point scale. Next, inmate crowding tolerance was assessed using a housing preference and a tolerance test. Finally, inmates were asked to complete a detailed questionnaire about their perceptions of prison housing, their mood state, and background.

Housing evaluation was assessed by asking inmates to rate their room, cubicle, cell, or dormitory on 7-point scale using the following six dimensions: 'good–bad, unattractive–attractive, right number of people–too many people, unpleasant–pleasant, well arranged–poorly arranged, and uncomfortable–comfortable. Mood state was similarly assessed. Inmates were asked how they had felt in the past week along the following dimensions: relaxed–bored, wide awake–sleepy, happy–unhappy, tough–weak, satisfied–unsatisfied, stimulated–relaxed, important–unimportant, and tense–calm. In some of the later visits, two questions about control over one's situation and over others in the institution and four questions covering the degree of choice about life in prison were added. Based on the factor analyses, the items of these various subscales were added to form summary scores (room rating, control, choice, and mood). In the case of the mood scales, two items (stimulated–relaxed and tense–calm) appeared

TABLE 4–1. List of criterion variables

Illness rate
Perceived crowding (1 = low, 4 = high)
Room rating (6 scales, high = positive)
Systolic blood pressure
Diastolic blood pressure
Mood (6 scales, high = positive)
Tense/stimulated (2 scales, high = positive)
Crowding complaints (high = more)
Other complaints (high = more)
Choice (3 scales, high = positive)
Control (2 scales, high = positive)
Sleep problems (0 = no, 1 = yes)
Headache problems (0 = no, 1 = yes)
Tolerance (high = more tolerance)

TABLE 4–2. List of predictor variables

Parent's occupation (1 = nonskilled, 2 = skilled, 3 = professional)
Parent's high school (0 = not graduated, 1 = graduate)
Homesize (high = more people in home)
Last grade completed in school
Hometown as child (1 = small, 2 = large)
Hometown as adult (1 = small, 2 = large)
Prior commitments (0–3)
Duration of prior commitments (weeks)
Custody (1 = closed, 2 = medium, 3 = minimum, 4 = community)
Months left to serve
Weeks in housing
Weeks in prison
Weeks in present sentence
Age

to represent a separate factor and were summed to form a separate mood score. Only three choice items were used for the summary score, since one item (recreation) was used for only a few visits.

Additional items pertained to trouble with sleeping and problems with headaches. Inmates were also asked what bothered them most about their housing conditions. Answers to these questions were coded as crowding-related or noncrowding-related. A copy of the questionnaire is in Appendix A, and a summary of the main items is in Table 4–1.

The questionnaire was also used to obtain background information. This was supplemented by information gleaned directly from prison records. A summary of the primary items of the information obtained is in Table 4–2. In addition, inmates were asked about their involvement in various prison activities (e.g., club, educational). Since this information did not appear to be related to prison crowding, we will not discuss results for the activity measures.

Data about illness complaints were obtained from medical clinic records. The data and type of complaint were noted for each inmate during the period in which they were residents in their latest housing units. Such data were gathered for up to a 6-month period. We derived a measure of total illness complaints per week during this period of time. We also analyzed separately the illness rates for the period of time after the residents had been in their housing unit for 6 weeks. This measure was designed to minimize carryover effects from a prior unit and allow a sufficient period of time for the development of health problems related to housing.

The major measures employed in our program were perceived crowding, blood pressure, illness complaints, disciplinary infractions, housing unit evaluation, mood state, and perception of control. We will discuss our results for these measures for the six federal prisons employed. The major focus will be on results related to type of inmate housing. Subsequent chapters will deal with additional findings regarding health, tolerance, and influence of inmate characteristics.

Texarkana—Singles, Doubles, and Dorms

While we were examining crowding in various prisions, we decided that obtaining additional data from the Texarkana prison was also warranted. We had never fully explored the wide range of housing available there. We made two large-scale visits to this medium security institution. During the first visit, population was near its 780 inmate capacity (710), while at the second visit, population had declined to 510. Inmates were assigned to housing units on the basis of availability, but typically they were initially assigned to dormitories and moved to doubles and singles on a seniority basis (see Fig. 4–2 and 4–3). Since the data for the first and second visit were comparable and the measures employed for the second visit were more extensive, only the results for the second visit will be reported.

The results were quite consistent with those of our prior studies (Table 4–3). Specific comparisons using analysis of covariance to control for weeks in prison, custody level, and months left to serve yielded a variety of interesting results. Regular dorms housing 27 to 29 inmates were rated as more crowded and were associated with negative housing evaluations, negative mood reactions, and higher illness complaint rates than singles. However, while doubles were rated more negatively than singles and were associated with a more negative mood state, they did not show elevated illness complaint rates. Large singles with 66 sq ft did not yield strongly positive reactions compared with regular singles with 54 sq ft. Thus again, it appears that the most important factor is the number of people in one's housing unit rather than the space. The low levels of space in doubles were associated with negative psychological reactions, but not differences in illness. A space variation of 12 ft in singles had little effect.

Does this pattern of results indicate that the number of residents is the

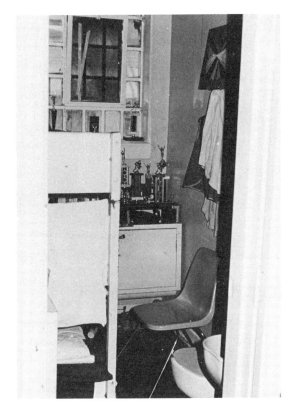

FIGURE 4–2. A typical double cell in a federal prison.

FIGURE 4–3. One of the dormitories at Texarkana FCI.

Results for housing type at Texarkana FCI

Variables	Regular singles 54 sq ft N[a] = 43/50	Large singles 66 sq ft N = 30/32	Doubles 27 sq ft N = 35/40	Regular dorms 34/35 sq ft N = 31/45	Special dorms 51 sq ft N = 24/32
Perceived crowding[b]	1.8	1.5	2.9	3.2	2.5
Summary room rating (6 scales)	25.8	28.2	15.6	11.8	16.0
Mood	23.4	21.9	19.4	17.4	18.6
Control	7.9	8.5	6.3	6.9	8.1
Illness rate (> 6 weeks)	.14	.14	.08	.33	.23
Weeks in prison	46.8	64.7	42.9	42.6	28.1
Custody level	2.7	2.7	2.7	2.6	2.0
Months left to serve	16.1	11.3	21.5	11.2	15.3

Notes: [a] N is the number of subjects in each housing type. It varies because all of the information was not obtained from all of the inmates.

[b] A high score means more crowding; for the other questionnaire items, high is positive. Significant effects ($p < .05$) were obtained for all of these variables when comparing regular singles, doubles, and regular dorms. The information on the large singles and special dorm is presented for comparison purposes (see text).

only important factor? Several other findings suggest that this is not the case. Texarkana contained several architecturally "special" dorms that housed about 10 more inmates than the regular dorms, but were a little more spacious and were segmented into three visually separated bays. The residents of the special dorms also had mostly single bunks in contrast to

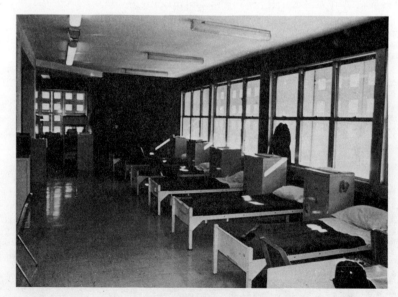

FIGURE 4–4. One segment of the "special" dorms at Texarkana FCI.

the double-bunking of the regular dorms (Fig. 4–4). Relative to
dorms, the special dorms were rated more positively and had lowe
complaint rates. This finding indicates that factors that increase priv
an open dorm can make living with a large number of inmates more toຝᵤᵢ-
able. The importance of provision for privacy in open dorms is further
demonstrated in the results for two other prisons, which are discussed next.

El Reno—Singles, Doubles, and Cubicles

The data from Texarkana provided evidence that doubles may be disliked
as compared with singles, but they may not lead to elevated illness complaint rates. El Reno FCI provided an opportunity to assess the generality
of these results, since most of the housing there consists of singles and
doubles. El Reno is also a medium security institution which housed about
1,200 residents with an average age of 30 years.

We examined inmates in four buildings. Two of these buildings consisted

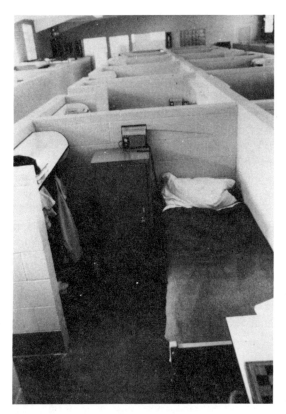

FIGURE 4–5. A dorm with concrete cubicles currently employed at El Reno FCI and
other federal prisons.

TABLE 4–4. Housing results for El Reno[a]

Variables	Housing				Significance levels
	Singles		Doubles		
	Room	Cube	Room	Cube	
Number of subjects	42	52	49	40	
Perceived crowding[b]	2.2	2.6	3.4	3.2	$p < .001$
Room rating[c]	16.5	16.9	10.7	12.8	$p < .001$
Nonaggressive infractions	.05	.09	.40	.28	$p < .01$
Systolic blood pressure	114.9	109.9	115.6	111.6	$p < .02$
Weeks in prison	67.7	51.4	31.6	24.5	$p < .001$
Weeks in housing	27.4	31.1	8.0	10.8	$p < .001$
Custody	2.5	2.1	1.9	1.8	$p < .02$

Notes: [a] Significant main effects for doubles were obtained for each of these variables except for blood pressure, which had a main effect for type of room.
[b] High is negative.
[c] High is positive.

of single and double rooms, while the other half housed single and double cubicles. The cubicles were placed in what was formerly an open dormitory. The cubicles were 5 ft 6 in. high and enclosed a 7×7 ft area. The cubicles provided some storage and writing space. Each wing housed 48 cubicles, with 19 containing double bunks (Fig. 4–5). The rooms measured 5 ft 10 in. $\times$ 10 ft, and were clustered in groups of 35 in the two wings of each floor. One building with rooms contained Youth Corrections Act inmates. The other buildings received inmates on a random basis, with new inmates typically assigned to doubles.

The residents of doubles rated their housing more negatively and had higher rates of disciplinary infractions. Residents of cubicles had lower blood pressures than residents of rooms (Table 4–4). When rooms and cubicles were compared (for both singles and doubles), it was evident that these two different housing types yield essentially the same reactions. Residents of singles had been in the institution and their housing longer than residents of doubles, and had a less severe custody level. When one controls for these factors, only the effect of nonaggressive infractions is significantly reduced ($p < .10$). However, if one examines only those inmates who have been in the institution for at least 6 weeks (allowing for greater comparability between the two groups), the effect on infractions remains strong ($p < .01$).

The El Reno study supports that of Texarkana in that doubles are a source of negative reactions but not increased illness rates.[1] Cubicles that

---

[1] In a previous paper, we reported a difference in illness rates between singles and doubles for this prison. These results were limited only to those inmates living in cells.

TABLE 4–5. Housing results for Danbury FCI[a]

Variables	Singles	Cubicles	Open dorms
Number of occupants	1	1	54/65
Space (sq ft per person)	48/60	50	49/59
Number of subjects	60/75	20/24	47/63
Perceived crowding[b]	1.5	1.5	3.2
Summary room rating[c]	26.1	30.8	14.0
Mood[c]	25.4	24.0	21.1
Tense-stimulated[c]	9.0	9.3	7.7
Illness (> 6 weeks)	.08	.18	.16
Weeks in prison	71.9	61.4	28.3
Weeks in housing	21.3	14.8	14.7
Custody	3.2	3.5	2.6

Notes: [a] All effects of housing at $p = .001$, except for weeks in housing ($p < .05$) and illness ($p < .002$).
[b] A high score is more crowded.
[c] A high score is more positive.

provide less complete privacy than rooms elicited reactions similar to that of the rooms. These findings again emphasize the importance of privacy. Doubles reduce privacy and hence elicit negative reactions. Cubicles allow inmates to achieve a measure of privacy in open dorms and hence yield reactions similar to those of regular rooms.

Danbury—Singles, Cubicles, and Dorms

The El Reno study indicated that partitions may greatly reduce the negative impact of dormitory housing. Yet in this study, no open dormitories were available for comparison. Danbury FCI did provide such an opportunity. Danbury is a medium security prison where the average age of inmates is 36 years. At the time of our visit, it held 669 inmates. It contained single rooms, cubicles, and open dormitories with 54 or 65 inmates, with some variation in space within the singles (48 versus 60 sq ft) and dorms (49 versus 59 sq ft per inmate). The cubicles were similar in design to those at El Reno and provided 50 sq ft of space. It should also be noted that different housing units varied in the programs to which inmates were assigned. For singles, these units were industry, alcohol abuse, and life skills. In dorms, inmates were assigned to industry or alcohol abuse, and one unit of the open dorms and the cubicle dorm contained inmates not assigned to a program.

The results of the Danbury study indicated that inmates react similarly to both singles and cubicles and relatively negatively to open dormitories. Analyses of the illness data revealed that both the cubicle and the open dorms were associated with elevated illness complaint rates relative to singles (Table 4–5). Thus our results should be viewed with caution. The

TABLE 4–6. Effects of housing across different types of units at
Danbury FCI

| | Variables | |
Housing	Perceived crowding	Illness (> 6 weeks)
Singles		
Industry unit	1.6	.09
Life skills unit	1.5	.03
Alcohol unit	1.5	.08
Dormitories		
Industry unit	3.2	.14
Unassigned unit	3.6	.12
Alcohol unit	2.8	.20
Cubicles		
Unassigned unit	1.5	.23

fact that all of the cubicles came from one unit raises the possibility that
the results for the cubicles are subject to unique events associated with that
unit. However, the psychological evaluation data indicate that inmates at
Danbury, like those at El Reno, find cubicles similar in desirability to
rooms.

As in other prisons, inmates in differing housing conditions also differed
in several other characteristics—length of time in prison, length of time
in housing, and custody level. We have reported only those effects that
remained significant after controlling for these factors by analyses of covariance. Additional analyses indicated that program assignment did not
significantly influence inmate reactions to different types of housing (see
Table 4–6). There was evidence that minor variations in space can affect
psychological reactions. The more spacious dorms (59 sq ft/inmate) were
rated more positively than less spacious dorms (49 sq ft/inmate), and the
more spacious singles (60 sq ft/inmate) were rated more positively than
less spacious singles.

Atlanta—Multiple-Occupant Cells

All of the studies reported thus far (except for the state prison study) have
been done in medium security federal prisons. Much of our focus has been
on comparing dormitories with single or double cells and and cubicles. This
comparison involves a substantial variation in social density (1 and 2 versus
28 or more). However, prison housing in state prisons and maximum security prisons often involves placing inmates in multiple-occupant cells housing up to eight inmates. Do variations in social density in this range produce significant differences in inmate reactions? Our state prison study

TABLE 4–7. Effects of multiple-occupant housing in Atlanta

Variables	Housing units					Significance levels
Social density	1	3	4	5	6	
Space (sq ft per person)	54	58	44	35	29	
Number of subjects	27/54	18/20	39/40	26/27	8/9	
Perceived crowding[a]	1.4	2.4	2.1	3.1	3.3	$p<.001$
Summary room ratings[b]	21.7	18.6	19.0	15.8	15.0	$p<.01$
Illness (rate per week)[c]	0.11	0.12	0.19	0.19	0.20	$p<.05$
Diastolic blood pressure	60.6	52.7	65.7	64.8	52.4	$p<.001$
Custody[d]	1.3	1.6	1.7	1.6	1.3	$p<.01$

Notes: [a] The higher the number, the more crowded.
[b] The higher the number, the more positive.
[c] The significance level in this case is for a comparison of singles versus multiple-occupant housing.
[d] A high score means for favorable custody.

comparing doubles with three- and six-man cells and our comparisons of singles and doubles suggest that variations in the number of inmates sharing a cell will have a strong impact.

The Atlanta Federal Penitentiary provided an opportunity to further evaluate this issue since it housed inmates in 50 sq ft single cells or 176 sq ft cells with 3, 4, 5, or 6 inmates. The Atlanta penitentiary is a large, old maximum security institution. At the time of our study, it held about 1,700 inmates with an average age of 37 years. Today this institution is used for detaining Cubans with criminal records who entered this country in the 1970s.

Consistent with expectations from our prior studies, increasing the number of inmates in a cell increased the negative psychological reactions as well as illness complaint rates in those who had been in their housing more than 6 weeks. Diastolic blood pressure also varied significantly among housing units, being elevated in the four- and five-man units (Table 4–7). There was also a difference in custody level among the housing types, but controlling for this by analysis of covariance did not appreciably affect the results.

Overall Analyses of Housing Type

Although we have discussed the effects of housing type for different prisons, the three housing types of singles, doubles, and dorms were represented in a number of prisons. To gain a clearer picture of the effects of these housing types, the combined data for six federal prisons were analyzed (Table 4–8).

These analyses show again that dormitories and doubles are perceived as more crowded than singles and are rated more negatively on various dimensions. Dormitory residents have higher rates of illness complaints

TABLE 4–8. The effects of different housing types for six federal prisons

Variables	Single	Double	Dorm	F value	p value
Total illness rate	.18	.17	.26	4.10	.02
Illness rate (>6 weeks)	.11	.15	.21	8.30	.001
Perceived crowding[a]	1.83	3.13	3.08	113.67	.001
Room rating	23.42	12.79	14.18	80.90	.001
Tense-stimulated	24.22	20.40	19.78	9.08	.001
Perceived control	8.12	6.53	7.08	3.28	.04
Headache	.38	.41	.74	13.67	.001
Age	34.89	32.59	32.63	5.16	.01
Last grade in school	10.46	10.26	9.81	3.35	.05
Prior commitments	2.10	1.11	1.82	8.21	.001
Months left to serve	21.19	17.93	16.69	3.63	.03
Duration of previous confinement	123.39	94.67	84.59	4.34	.01
Weeks on present sentence	92.21	54.91	46.05	32.23	.001
Weeks in present prison	69.55	34.63	28.85	63.54	.001
Weeks in present housing	27.06	17.11	18.73	6.64	.01
Custody level	2.14	2.29	2.39	13.87	.001

Note: [a] A high score is negative; for the other questionnaire measures a high score is positive.

than do residents of doubles or singles. Feelings of control over others were relatively lower in doubles and dorms, and mood state (tense-stimulated feeling scores) were more negative in the doubles and dorms than in the singles. Dormitory residents also reported more problems with headaches. These findings indicate that both doubles and dormitories are similarly negative in their impact on feelings of crowding, evaluation of housing, mood state, and feelings of control. However, dormitory residents had higher illness complaint rates and more problems with headaches than did the residents of singles and doubles. Thus, although the residents of doubles and dorms may find their housing similarly unpleasant, additional demands of dormitory living may result in an increase in more serious stress-related conditions such as illness and headaches.

As can be seen toward the bottom of Table 4–8, residents of the three housing types also differ in some of the characteristics we previously examined. Differences in reactions to housing may be partially attributable to these factors. To assess this problem, a regression analysis was done in which all of the predictor variables used in the previous regression analyses were entered simultaneously with two housing contrasts (singles versus doubles and dorms versus singles and doubles). This analysis indicates that the housing effects are generally not attributable to the influence of the other predictor variables (Table 4–9). Housing effects for the tense-stimulated and control items were not obtained because of the similarity of the results in the doubles and dorms for these items. It should also be noted that an effect of housing on blood pressure was obtained. This effect apparently reflects the slightly elevated blood pressure of dormitory resi-

TABLE 4–9. Contribution of predictor and housing variables in mu[...] analyses for singles, doubles, and dorms in six federal prisons

Criterion variable	Predictor variable	Beta	Significance		
Total illness	Months left	.11	.03		
	Weeks in prison	−.13	.05		
	Dorms/rest	−.11	.04	.oo	440
Perceived crowding	Custody	−.15	.001		
	Parent's occupation	.15	.01		
	Weeks in prison	.12	.03		
	Singles/doubles	−.41	.001		
	Dorms/rest	−.26	.001	.33	436
Room rating	Age	.15	.001		
	Custody	.13	.01		
	Parent's occupation	−.10	.04		
	Singles/doubles	.37	.001		
	Dorms/rest	.26	.001	.31	436
Systolic blood pressure	Age	.23	.001		
	Weeks committed	−.11	.05		
	Custody	.12	.03		
	Parent's high school	.12	.02		
	Dorms/rest	−.10	.05	.12	436
Diastolic blood pressure	Age	.42	.001		
	Weeks committed	−.18	.001		
	Custody	.10	.04		
	Weeks in prison	.12	.03		
	Dorms/rest	−.09	.04	.28	461
Illness (> 6 weeks)	Dorms/rest	−.20	.01	.06	279
Mood	Age	.22	.02	.15	155
Tense-stimulated	Age	.19	.04		
	Priors	−.19	.05	.18	155
Control	None			.08	155
Headaches	Dorms/rest	−.33	.001	.23	147

dents (systolic, 118.7 versus 117.8 mm Hg; diastolic, 62.8 versus 61.5 mm Hg), which becomes significant when controlling for other variables.

Time in Housing

The amount of time spent in a particular housing unit may influence a person's reactions to this unit. One of our studies found some evidence for increased sensitivity to crowding with increased time of exposure to such conditions. Thus, in the dormitories, and possibly doubles, increased time in housing may be associated with increasingly negative reactions. Yet little support for this hypothesis is evident. In fact, the most consistent result was a lowering of illness complaint rates with increased time in housing,

TABLE 4–10. Effects of time (in weeks) in housing

Housing types	1–5	6–10	11–15	16 or more
Singles				
Perceived crowding	1.7	1.9	1.6	1.6
Room rating	25.6	26.2	27.4	25.5
Illness	.31	.27	.23	.14
Control	7.8	8.4	8.0	8.6
Doubles				
Perceived crowding	3.1	3.1	3.3	2.9
Room rating	14.3	13.8	13.0	13.4
Illness	.38	.17	.21	.16
Systolic blood pressure	112.4	121.1	121.2	120.9
Dorms				
Perceived crowding	3.1	3.2	3.2	3.1
Room rating	12.1	12.5	14.4	14.5
Illness	.81	.32	.29	.18
Control	6.2	5.8	8.9	7.3

especially in dormitories (Table 4–10). This suggests that initial exposure to a particular housing unit, with its associated exposure to new inmates (in the dorm or hallway), is associated with a relatively high level of stress and illness. Continued time in housing with the associated increase in familiarity with nearby inmates may lead to a lowering of stress and illness. The fact that the various housing evaluation and mood scales were not related to the length of time in housing would seem to suggest that these may be sensitive to a different aspect of the housing environment. One of the questionnaire items, perceived control, did yield an effect of time in that feelings of control increased over time in the dorms. This is of interest since perceived control may tap the experience of increased familiarity and social structure, which may be associated with increased time in housing unit, especially in dormitories.

Jail Studies

While most of our data on crowding in correctional institutions have come from prisons, we have been able to obtain data from several jails. Jails house inmates for relatively short periods of time, and though they may be quite crowded, it may be difficult to observe health-related consequences of crowding in the limited incarceration periods. However, in one of our initial studies, we did find some evidence of elevated illness complaints in crowded jail housing (Paulus et al., 1975). McCain and Paulus (1982) were able to examine the effects of crowding in three different jail facilities (see also Paulus & McCain, 1983).

One of the jails was a minimum security institution, formerly a hospital, with about 285 inmates. Inmates were housed in rooms of varying size (83 to 299 sq ft) and number of residents (one to six). The rooms had no doors and opened onto long corridors. This institution provided a unique opportunity to assess the effects of social density across a wide range of spatial densities (36 to 260 sq ft/person). In our prisons, range of spatial density within and across housing types has been somewhat limited.

Inmates were asked to rate their living quarters along various dimensions and had their blood pressures taken. It was found that rooms with large numbers of residents elicited relatively more negative reactions, but did not increase blood pressure (Paulus & McCain, 1983). Regression analyses comparing the relative influence of the number of residents and the amount of space indicated that only social density contributed to the room evaluations.

A similar study was done at a medium security jail in which inmates were housed in cells in groups ranging from 2 to 24 inmates. Cells were grouped in units, with free movement within these units. Generally, inmates living in high social density cells also had greater numbers of inmates in their units. Space per person was fairly comparable across housing types. Cells with eight or more inmates were rated more negatively than those with only two inmates.

In a third jail, we compared four- and eight-man cells, but found no differences in inmate reactions. This may have been related to the greater amount of space available in units with eight-man cells. Not surprisingly, units housing violent inmates produced greater feelings of crowding and more reports of sleeping problems.

The jail studies are consistent with our prison studies in showing that social density, but not spatial density, is an important factor in inmate reactions to their housing. We failed to find differences in blood pressure, and this is consonant with the lack of blood pressure effects in most of our prison studies. In contrast to the prison findings, no effects of housing on illness complaint rates were observed. It is possible that the limited length of time inmates are typically confined to jails is not sufficient to produce health-related consequences of housing density in most cases.

Summary

We have described in some detail the results of our studies on prison and jail housing. These results paint a fairly consistent picture of prison crowding. Increasing the number of residents in a housing unit increases negative psychological and physical reactions in inmates. The most important factor appears to be the number of residents sharing a space and not the amount of space available. Providing cubicles in open dormitories reduces the negative impact of living there. Apparently being able to have a place to call one's own and being able to limit visual and physical access of others to this place is important to inmate satisfaction, adjustment, and health.

The results of our studies are consistent with those done by other researchers in prison and nonprison environments (see Chapters 2 and 3). For example, in regard to our finding on dormitory living, studies by D'Atri and colleagues in a state prison have shown that dorm inmates have higher blood pressures than single-cell inmates (D'Atri & Ostfeld, 1975). Our findings with cubicles have also been replicated. Gaes (1982) examined inmates living in open and cubicle areas of the same dormitories. Inmates residing in the open areas had more negative reactions and higher noncontagious illness complaint rates than those living in cubicles. Negative effects of social density in housing also have been demonstrated in such environments as naval ships (Dean, Pugh, & Gunderson, 1975), crowded residences (Gove et al., 1979), and college dormitories (Baum & Valins, 1979). The effects observed have ranged from negative environmental evaluations to impaired social behavior and health. Baum and Valins (1979) also found that the number of residents one has to contend with in one's living area, rather than space, is the important factor. Although our research has focused on a special population living under confined conditions, the results of our work are congruent with those derived from other populations and environments.

The influence of time in housing suggests some degree of adaptation in that illness complaints seem to decline with longer time in housing. Yet affective reactions and rating of the environment do not seem to change in this manner, suggesting that actual perception of the environment may not have changed. We did not observe sensitization or increased negative reactions over time on any measures. Such effects might be observed with the somewhat more volatile or violent populations found in many state prisons. With such populations, high density living conditions are even more likely to be associated with negative experiences, and adapation may be less likely.

5
Crowding and Health

Illness

Assuming that crowding induces psychological stress, one would expect manifestations of psychological stress to be evident in crowded prison environments. A variety of physiological changes are often associated with psychological stress, including changes that would be expected to express themselves in alterations in physical health. Numerous studies have demonstrated alterations in immune and cardiovascular functions in response to psychological stress (Elliott & Eisdorfer, 1982; Evans & Cohen, 1987). If crowding induces psychological stress, we reasoned that we should see expressions of this in health measures of inmates related to the degree of exposure to crowding. Consequently, we examined indices of inmate health that were obtainable in a prison setting. Many of our findings focused on illness complaints. Interpretation of illness complaints is not simple. For example, they may simply reflect attempts to gain attention, increased irritability, or sensitivity to somatic symptoms. However, the analyses to be presented suggest that illness complaints of prison inmates may be indicative of genuine physical pathology. This would be expected if indeed psychological stress is induced by crowding, since in other contexts, stress has been shown to affect physiological functions related to health and illness.

Illness complaint data were obtained directly from the medical files. We noted each complaint, its associated diagnosis by the medical doctor, and the date of occurrence. Each complaint that occurred while inmates were in their present housing unit was recorded for a period of up to 6 months (Table 5–1). Multiple complaints during a visit were coded as distinct complaints. The nature of each complaint was coded, and the resulting set of complaint types was subjected to a factor analysis to determine the degree

Verne Cox and Garvin McCain made significant contributions to this chapter. Much of the archival data were collected and analyzed by McCain. Gerald Gaes assisted in the detailed analyses of the illness data and the survey of physicians.

TABLE 5–1. Examples of the most frequent illness symptoms during prison health clinic visits (N = 1199)

Illness category	%
Venereal disease	.9
Chest pain	1.4
Virus, chills, fever	1.8
Headache	2.8
Nerves, psychoses	4.8
Gastrointestinal, stomach	4.8
Rhinitis, asthma	5.8
Foot, neck, shoulder, hip pain	6.1
Joints, bursitis, arthritis	6.3
Skin, subcutaneous problems	6.4
Injury, trauma	7.2
Eye, ear, nose, throat infections	8.4
Cough, cold, flu	13.1

Note: The values are the percentage of complaints relative to the total number of complaints reported (N = 3426).

TABLE 5–2. Categories and weights of the four factor solution for illness data

	1	2	3	4
Eigen-value	6.98	1.78	1.72	1.27
	.29 Nerves, insomnia, anxiety, nightmares	.46 Venereal problems	.56 Miscellaneous	.47 Nerves, appetite, insomnia, nightmares
	.62 Headaches	.29 Psychotic symptoms	.39 Gas, constipation, bowels	
	.65 Problems of eye, ear, nose, or throat	.44 Circulation, heart	.84 Urine infection, gastrointestinal, kidney, liver	.80 Psychological, depression, schizophrenia
	.75 Rhinitis/sinitis, nasal	.42 Upper respiratory, allergy	.31 Back and neck pain	.32 Miscellaneous
	.30 Upper respiratory, breathing, allergy, hayfever	.32 Stomach, ulcer	.38 Chest pain	.28 Loss of appetite, nausea
	.29 Asthma	.64 Female problems	.46 Foot pain	.33 Gastrointestinal pain
	.64 Cough, cold, flu	.46 Joints, hernia	.62 Scrotum, penis, groin	.61 Malaise

TABLE 5–2. *Continued.*

	1	2	3	4
Eigen-value	6.98	1.78	1.72	1.27

1	2	3	4
.26 Gas, constipation, loss of appetite	.55 Bursitis, arthritis	.30 Illegible entry	.35 Swollen glands, bodyaches, chills, fever
.56 Vomiting, indigestion	.43 Dizziness, fainting		
.23 Joints, bones, limbs, hands, fingers, muscle spasms, hernia, hip, flank, shin and sidepain, tailbone	.66 Renew medication		
	.28 Illegible entry		
.26 Backpain			
.33 Malaise			
.42 Dizziness			
.65 Sweating, virus, bodyaches and pain, numbness, fever, chills, tired, weak, swollen glands			
.30 Scrotum, penis			

of commonality among the various complaints. This analysis yielded four factors (Table 5–2). Factor 1 appears to consist of a wide variety of complaints, many of which seem stress-related. Factor 2 encompasses primarily objective-verifiable symptomology. Factor 3 consists mainly of pain-related complaints. Factor 4 involves primarily psychological complaints. These scores were subjected to an analysis of variance to determine which set of illness complaints best differentiated among the three different types of housing (single cell, double cell, and dormitory). Significant effects were found only for Factors 2 and 3 (Table 5–3). It is interesting to note that Factor 2 consists mostly of objectively verifiable conditions, while Factor 3 includes many pain-related complaints. These results suggest that the ill-

−3. The effects of different housing types on illness

Variables	Single	Double	Dorm	F value	p value
Total illness rate (all complaints)	.18	.17	.26	4.10	.02
Factor 2 illness rate (verifiable)	.032	.041	.058	3.30	.04
Factor 3 illness rate (pain-related)	.052	.042	.091	6.85	.002
Verifiable and noncontagious illness rate	.025	.041	.054	5.95	.003

ness complaint effects we observed in our research reflect, in part, real physical pathology. This is consistent with evidence from other studies documenting the health-related effects of exposure to stressors (Cox et al., 1982).

To further evaluate the nature of illness complaints, physicians from three military clinics in the Washington, D.C. area were asked to rate the major illness symptoms along three dimensions: verifiability, contagiousness, and stress sensitivity. Using a criterion of 75% agreement, symptoms were categorized as contagious, stress-sensitive, and verifiable. Most agreement was 90% or higher. An analysis of the relationship of housing type to the three illness categories and a combined verifiable-noncontagious category revealed a significant effect for the verifiable-noncontagious category (Table 5–3). This analysis strengthened the conclusion based on the earlier factor analysis. In both cases, symptoms characterized by high verifiability most clearly differentiated among housing conditions (Paulus & Gaes, 1986).

The effects for the verifiable categories suggest that crowded dormitory living has an impact on physical health. This category of complaint allows the physician to assess the validity of the complaint. Our examination of clinic logs suggests entries of this type reflected verification by physicians since a specific diagnosis and prescription for medication or treatment was often part of the clinic log entry. The effect on pain-related complaints is also consistent with a stress-based interpretation of the illness effects in dormitories, since four of the eight complaint types in this category (gas/constipation, back/neck pain, chest pain, and gastrointestinal) were rated by physicians as likely to be stress-related. It might be noted that earlier analyses indicated that reports of headache, another stress-related category, were also elevated in dormitories.

The failure to find significant effects for other illness categories is also of interest. Contagious illness may not be related to housing type because of the high level of contact among inmates in areas outside housing quarters. It should be noted that Gaes (1982) reported that residents of open dormitories have elevated noncontagious illness complaints, but not contagious illness complaints when compared with inmates housed in cubicles. In prisons and jails where inmates are confined to their quarters most of

TABLE 5–4. Mean levels of reported crowding, control, symptom distre' ary catecholamines

Variables	Housing		
	Single	Cubicle	Dormitory
Perceived crowding	1.6	2.8	3.2
Perceived control	5.1	4.4	4.5
Symptoms	31.2	37.0	36.4
Epinephrine (ng/ml)	3.2	3.7	7.4
Norepinephrine (ng/ml)	17.6	21.9	45.2

the day, contagious complaints may be elevated in more crowded housing. The lack of a relationship between stress-sensitive and psychological complaints and housing may reflect general reactivity to prison stressors in general.

Urine Chemistry Correlates of Stress and Housing

The illness data provide strong support for the conclusion that dormitory crowding is a stressor and is detrimental to health. The relationship of housing to physiological indicators of stress has been examined by investigation of the relationship of autonomic nervous system responses to crowding and by examination of urine chemistry correlates of adrenal catecholamines. D'Atri (1975) and D'Atri and Ostfeld (1975) found that dormitories were associated with elevated blood pressure as compared with single-cell housing. More recently, Schaeffer, Paulus, Baum, and Gaes (in press) examined urinary catecholamine levels as an index of stress engendered by different degrees of crowding. These investigators examined urine samples from 80 inmates housed in single cells, single cubicles, and dormitories. Additional measures were obtained for feelings of crowding, control, and illness. As seen in Table 5–4, cubicle and dormitory residents felt more crowded than residents of single-occupant housing. Urinary epinephrine and norepinephrine levels were elevated in dormitories relative to single-occupant housing. Dormitory and cubicle residents had spent less time in their current housing and had served fewer weeks of their sentence than singles residents. However, additional analyses indicated that these factors did not account for the results. While these data suggest greater psychological stress related to dormitories, the illness complaint data were highest for cubicles. Sample sizes were smaller than the ones previously used for investigation of illness complaints. It may be that the urinary catecholamine levels are a more sensitive measure of stress than illness complaints, and that a large sample size is required to detect a systematic relationship between housing and illness complaints.

The health data gathered from individual inmates have demonstrated that crowding is related to various indices of health. However, one might still question the severity of the observed effects. Do elevations in clinic visits and various physiological indices indicate a serious health problem? This, of course, depends on one's criteria. It is difficult to compare our results with data gathered from other populations because of the idiosyncracies of prison health care. Thus the only statements one can make with confidence are those about the relative impact of different housing types within the prison population.

Archival Data on Health and Maladaptive Behavior

There is another important source of information about health-related problems that can help illuminate the extent to which crowded prison conditions are associated with physical and mental pathology—data on serious health-related incidents such as natural deaths and suicides from prison archives. Deriving meaningful data from such archives is an inherently difficult problem. Data on illness, headaches, sleeplessness, and blood pressure are ordinarily short-term and can be collected either directly from the inmate or inmate records. The researcher can determine what data are to be collected, the number of cases, and how sampling is to be structured. In contrast, archival data have to be gathered when and where it is available. Further, the incidence of events such as psychiatric commitments and deaths tends to be rather low so that relatively long time periods and/ or large samples are not only desirable, but necessary. Our rationale for collecting archival data was that crowding could produce stress and that prolonged stress could lead to serious physical and psychological consequences. Presumably, the most serious consequences of crowding-induced stress could not be seen except over an extended period of time.

We have used two major approaches in evaluating the relationship of crowding archival health data—assessing the impact of changes in population over time, and assessing differences between large and small institutions within a particular prison system. Even when institutions are equally crowded, our theoretical notions regarding crowding assume that because of greater social density, larger institutions would yield relatively greater stress and consequently a greater incidence of health-related problems. It was presumed that an increased population within a prison would be related to greater degrees of exposure to crowded conditions and unwanted interactions within the living quarters and/or in common use areas. In addition, institution size provides for more potential and actual interactions, regardless of the types of housing. There are, however, a large number of problems one confronts in dealing with such archival data. Variations or changes in recordkeeping and in the nature of the population and the effects of particular administrators or administrative policies are all potential sources of problems in collecting and interpreting archival data.

Our efforts to avoid or compensate for these possible sources of error or confusion took several lines. First, we tried to become thoroughly familiar with the systems or institutions involved by collecting background data and visiting some or all of the institutions involved (39 in all). Second, we obtained data for the longest period possible to minimize the potential impact of temporary effects from extraneous sources. The resultant periods of time ranged from 4 to 16 years. Third, in a number of cases, we collected data on several different measures such as suicides and natural deaths. Fourth, we obtained data from different systems to avoid situations that might be peculiar to a given system. Fifth, we looked at changes in population over time, as well as comparing large and small institutions within a given system. Sixth, we usually tried various combinations of institutions to avoid the possibility that one institution was distorting the results. None of the combinations changed the direction of the results in any of the analyses reported. Seventh, when possible, we obtained data on factors such as age, nature of offense, guard-inmate ratio, ethnic-racial identification, and changes in facilities to attempt to understand or control for variables not related to the effects of crowding. By using these approaches, we hoped to limit or evaluate the possibility that temporary or noncrowding-related conditions would affect our results. If we had only one short-term measure at one institution or even an entire system, it would be relatively easy to speculate or even find some evidence for alternate explanations such as changes in age composition of the population. With additional sites, measures, knowledge of background factors, and long periods of time, such explanations generally can be ruled out.

We have collected archival data from a number of systems and, in some cases, from more than one site within a system. Data were collected during several separate visits at some of these sites. The main prison systems included in our study were in Illinois and Texas. A brief description of some of the systems may be helpful in putting our results in perspective.

In 1977, 85% of the inmates in Illinois were mostly housed in institutions built between 1860 and 1934. Housing conditions varied widely, with cells or rooms housing one to nine inmates, and with many different kinds of dorms. There were 10 institutions, ranging in population from 320 to 2,600, with about 67% of the inmates in large units. The total system population was about 10,500. Oklahoma was one of the smaller systems we visited, with a population of about 3,500 in 1977. Most housing was in cells or rooms of one to four inmates, with some dormitories. Population per prison ranged from 400 to 1,400, with only one large unit.

The Texas system has been of particular interest to us because of its size and homogeneity. It is one of the largest state systems, with about 38,000 inmates. As of 1984, all institutions in Texas were rated as maximum security. With very few exceptions, there were only two types of housing—double cells of 45 sq ft and dormitories. At the beginning of the data period (1968), there were 15 institutions, and at the end (1984) there were 26. Institutions ranged in population from about 750 to 2,600 in 1977.

In discussing our wide range of archival results, we will first present the findings for changes in population and then for size of the institution. Within each of these categories, findings for specific health-related categories will be discussed separately.

Changes in Population

Death Rates

Obviously, one of the most important health indicators is the rate of natural deaths in a population. Most prisons keep careful records of deaths that occur within the institution. We obtained these records and/or death certificates from a number of institutions.

Our first data of this type came from Menard Psychiatric Prison in Illinois (Paulus et al., 1978). We obtained information about deaths and population for a period of 16 years. The Menard data consisted of a combination of natural and violent deaths, which could not be separated. As seen in Figure 5–1, as population increased, death rates increased, and then decreased as population decreased. Deaths rates were about 10 times higher at the highest populations as compared with the lowest. The changes in death rates lagged behind population changes. This was the expected result, based on our assumption that at least some effects of crowding require a period of time before they can be detected. This should

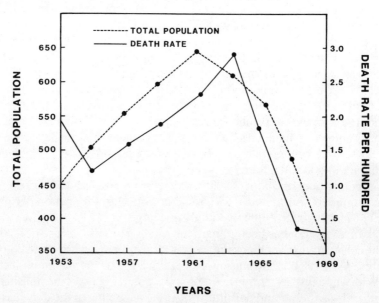

FIGURE 5–1. Changes in population and death rates for a psychiatric institution (adapted from Paulus et al., 1978).

be particularly true in the case of deaths from natural causes, sin
take some time for stress-related effects of changes in popula
come evident. It should be noted that this population was made
of older inmates. Older men may be more susceptible to the heal
effects of crowding (Herzog, Levy, & Verdonk, 1977).

Mortality data from the entire Illinois prison system for a period of eight
years were also obtained. These data allowed for specific examination of
natural deaths. In the high population years (7,900 to 9,000 inmates)
compared with the low population years (5,800 to 7,100 inmates), death
rates—including those from diseases of the circulatory system—were
significantly higher for those over 45 years of age (cf. Paulus et al., 1978).

Similar findings have been obtained in the Texas prison system. The
population in the Texas Department of Corrections (TDC) rose from
about 15,000 in 1971 to about 24,000 in 1978. During that period, housing
facilities increased about 30%. For each reported death, we obtained the
inmate's name, identification number, date of birth, cause of death, racial
identification, and unit of assignment. For seven of these years, we also
had a copy of all death certificates. Data on total population of the system,
age, racial breakdown, and individual unit populations were obtained from
TDC official sources. Our analyses indicated that deaths from natural
causes for inmates older than 50 years of age increased much more rapidly
than did population changes. The population increased slightly by over
90%, while the death rates increased by over 200% (McCain et al., 1980).

Suicides, Attempted Suicides, and Psychiatric Commitments

Although stress can have a direct effect on physical health, it may also have
dramatic effects on mental health (Elliott & Eisdorfer, 1982). One rough
measure of mental health in a prison population is the number of inmates
committed for psychiatric care. Specific policies and facilities may differ
from one prison system to another. However, within a particular prison
system, the relationship of psychiatric commitments to changes in population and institution size may be informative. Another dramatic measure of
mental health available in prison records is suicide. This measure is presumably influenced less by differences in institutional procedures than are
psychiatric commitments.

From the Illinois system and other sources (Jacobs, 1977), we were able
to obtain information on psychiatric commitments from two large institutions, Stateville and Joliet, for the period 1953–1969. Psychiatric commitment rates were highly correlated with total population (Fig. 5–2). When
we compared the highest levels of population with the lowest, higher
population was associated with higher commitment rates ($p < .001$)
(Paulus et al., 1978).

Data from the TDC were combined with those from a Master's thesis by
Smith (1977) to obtain data on suicides for the period 1964–1978. Popula-

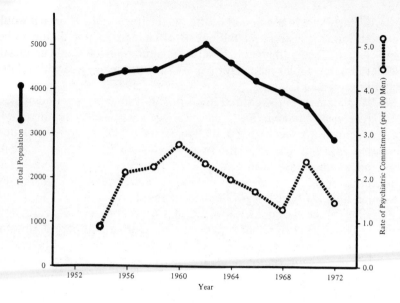

FIGURE 5–2. Changes in population and psychiatric commitments for two large prisons (adapted from Paulus et al., 1978).

tion increased by about 91%, while suicide rates increased about 1,000% (cf. McCain et al., 1980). We also found a systematic relationship between population level and rate of combined suicides and homicides in the Oklahoma prison system for the years 1973–1976 (Fig. 5–3). It can be seen that a moderate drop in population was associated with a rather dramatic decline in death rate.

Disciplinary Infractions

We were able to obtain data on disciplinary infractions in the Texas prison system during a period of 10 years when the population increased by 91% and housing increased by 30%. As can be seen in Figure 5–4, disciplinary infractions during this period increased by 400%.

The data on changes in population in institutions indicate that such changes can be associated with a variety of health problems. These results suggest that the stresses related to population pressures in high density institutions may result in a variety of pathological consequences. If population level is indeed important, one might expect that large institutions would be associated with more population-related stresses than would small ones. In large institutions, housing may not be more crowded, but external activity areas may be more densely populated. To examine this possibility, the impact of institution size was examined for a number of prison systems.

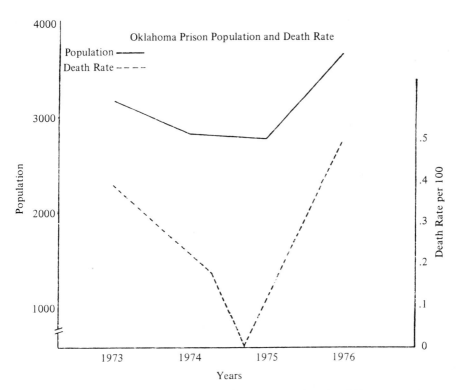

FIGURE 5–3. Changes in death rates and population for the Oklahoma prison system (adapted from McCain et al., 1980).

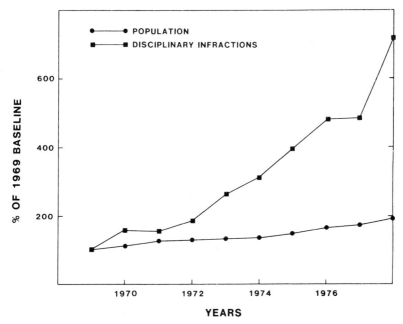

FIGURE 5–4. Changes in population and disciplinary infraction rates (from Cox et al., 1984).

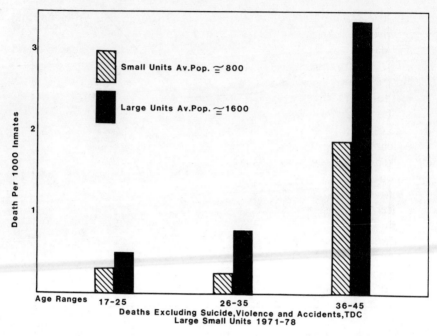

FIGURE 5–5. Institution size and death rates (from McCain et al., 1980).

Size of Institution

As with the changes in population measures, the size of an institution can be associated with a variety of factors other than differences in population. In many systems, large prisons have a greater variety of types of inmates than small ones, or small units may have special missions (e.g., medical or rehabilitative). However, in the Texas system, we found a broad range in size of institutions housing inmates under relatively similar conditions (maximum security) (McCain et al., 1980). In comparing small institutions (smaller than 1,200) with large ones (1,200 or larger), it was found that the psychiatric commitments were about 70% higher in the large institutions. Natural death rates were also elevated in large prisons, especially for the older inmates (Fig. 5–5). Thus the results for the size of institution are quite consistent with that of changes in population.

Summary

We have attempted to assess the effects of crowding on health and maladaptive behavior in a number of ways. Short-term effects have been examined in terms of illness complaints, headaches, and blood pressure. Long-term effects have included suicides, deaths from natural causes, and psychiatric commitments. The data presented here come from internal comparisons within institutions and entire systems.

The data form a coherent picture from many different measures and sources, and strongly support the conclusion that crowding does have important effects on physical and psychological health and behavior. With regard to illness, this conclusion must be tempered by the realization that most of our data provide only indirect evidence. Illness complaints may not represent actual pathology, although the evidence presented in the first part of the chapter helps bolster the assumption that real pathology is involved. Observed relationships between various indices of health and behavioral pathology and changes in population and institution size could be attributed to a host of factors other than crowding stress. We have dealt with this latter possibility in a number of ways.

In the case of the Texas system, we examined the role of age, ethnic identification, percentage of inmates committed for crimes against persons, and inmate–security personnel ratios. None of these appeared to account for the results of changes in population. Furthermore, race, ethnic group, age, and balance of cells and dorms did not appear to account for differences in size of institution. When possible, we have examined the influence of noncrowding variables in our other archival data sources and have avoided inclusion of unique institutions (e.g., hospital units). In spite of all of the potential problems with quality of archival data and its interpretation, the consistency of our results suggest that overall institution crowding may indeed have dramatic effects on health and maladaptive behavior. Gaes and McGuire (1985) similarly found that crowding was the most important predictor of assaults in federal prisons when compared with other variables such as age and staff–inmate ratio.

However, we cannot escape the fact that our archival data provide only circumstantial evidence. Ideally, direct measurements of physical health of prison inmates in institutions differing in size and population density should be taken. Also, a number of other investigators have reported a failure to observe crowding effects in their archival data (Carr, 1980; Ekland-Olson, 1986; Porporino & Dudley, 1984) or results inconsistent with ours (Innes, 1987). However, Porporino and Dudley (1984) examined only singles and doubles, and we have demonstrated only moderate differences between singles and doubles in our studies. Ekland-Olson used a space per person criterion, and Innes compared institutions in which inmates had less than 60 sq ft of space with those that were more spacious. We have already provided considerable evidence that it is the number of people one has to contend with in one's housing and external environment that may be the critical factor. Amount of space appears to be of secondary importance. In this light, it might be noted that most individual cells in the U.S. prisons provide less than 60 sq ft of space. The comparison used by Innes presumably included many single cells as high density housing.

It is thus quite evident that one simply cannot take any archival data set and expect to find crowding-related effects, especially if one uses density measures not very sensitive to the major crowding variable—the number of people in a housing unit. We have also failed to observe effects in a few instances. Based on our data from individual inmates and from the related crowding literature, we predict that comparisons that involve differences in social density in housing units (e.g., dorms) or in external activity areas would most likely be associated with effects on health and maladaptive behavior. Association of density with factors that increase the potential stresses involved in interactions in crowded environments (inmate turnover, high numbers of young-violent offenders, etc.) should further increase the likelihood of observing pathological effects (Ekland-Olson, 1986; Ellis, 1984). We will discuss this issue at greater length in Chapter 8.

6
Background and
Experiential Factors

The previous chapters have marshaled much evidence for the negative impact of crowding in prisons. Even though the findings are consistent, it is evident that not all inmates react negatively to living in crowded conditions. A small number actually prefer living in open dormitories rather than single cells. The same applies for other settings as well. Some people adjust better to crowded dormitories or to crowded cities than others. Many people, in fact, prefer living in crowded cities compared to small towns. What is the basis for such differences in preferences for and reactions to crowded environments? Past research has given us very few leads. There is some evidence that growing up in a large city or in a crowded home reduces the negative reactions to crowded environments (Baron et al., 1976; Wohlwill & Kohn, 1973). Yet no clear theoretical or empirical base exists to aid one's search for factors that might influence reactivity to crowding.

A variety of factors could account for individual variation in response to density. Much research suggests that one's reactivity to environmental stimuli diminishes with increased exposures (Gifford, 1987). This phenomenon is often called desensitization and is presumably independent of a person's behavioral reactions to the stimulus. From this perspective, increased exposure to dense conditions should decrease sensitivity to crowding. One would expect that those who have lived in crowded cities, homes, or prisons for considerable periods of time would be less affected by exposure to crowding than others. A perspective diametrically opposed to desensitization suggests that increased exposure to aversive stimuli may enhance one's sensitivity to these stimuli. This may be particularly true for stimuli that have an inherent quality of uncertainty (e.g., people). This possibility is suggested by the fact that many nonsocial stressors such as noise are associated with adaptation effects, while crowding is often associated with sensitization (Saegert, 1978; Paulus, 1980). For example, in one of our early studies of prison crowding, we found that inmates who had lived in a dormitory relatively longer than others demonstrated less tolerance of crowding on a simulated task. From this perspective it appears that exposure to crowding or deprivation of privacy may increase one's desire for low levels of crowding or high degrees of privacy.

Another basis for differences in reactions to crowding lies in the nature of experiences associated with being in crowded conditions. Those who have come to associate primarily positive experiences with crowded living conditions may not evidence negative reactions. In this category could be individuals who grew up with a large but harmonious and loving family (Herzog et al., 1977). Others may have experienced the congeniality of densely populated neighborhoods (cf. Michelson, 1976). The positive associations developed in these instances may be related to preferences for high-density living conditions which allow for spontaneous and frequent access to others.

A closely related phenomenon involves the coping experiences associated with crowded living conditions. Lazarus and Folkman (1984) emphasized the importance of coping responses in mediating reactions to stressful stimuli. Any technique designed to ameliorate the negative impact of the stressor is considered a coping response. If an individual is able to use one or more coping strategies successfully, the stress-producing impact of an aversive situation can be greatly reduced. Some background experiences may enable individuals to acquire crowding-relevant coping skills. Those who have successfully coped with crowding in the past will be better adjusted in crowded living conditions than those who have not been able to cope successfully. We did not explicitly assess past coping success, but certain predictions do seem tenable. Inmates who have spent a lot of time in prison may have learned to deal with many of the attendant problems related to crowding and show less crowding-related stress than those relatively new to prison life. Individuals who lived in crowded cities or shared bedrooms may have learned to deal effectively with crowded living conditions.

These predictions are quite general and presume success in dealing with past crowding. Of course since specific information about such past success was not available, our predictions must be considered to be quite tentative. Another problem with making predictions from this perspective is that coping specific to one particular situation may not transfer to a different setting (Lazarus & Folkman, 1984). So those who have learned to deal with city crowding may not be well prepared for living in crowded housing. Coping with city crowding may involve avoidance strategies (Milgram, 1970) that simply may not work in crowded living quarters. Obviously, future research will have to develop more precise measures of past coping behaviors and their efficacy and relate these to subsequent adjustment in a variety of situations. In the present study these perspectives were used to develop tentative predictions and to interpret the results.

The predictor variables used in our analyses were listed in Table 4–2. Factor analyses indicated some of these variables reflected somewhat similar factors. On this basis, we will deal with the influence of items that deal with a particular aspect of the individual's background or characteristics. One set of items seemed to reflect socioeconomic level: occupation of parent, completion of high school, homesize (the number of people in the home), and last grade completed in school. Another set of items reflected criminal history—custody level, number of prior commitments to prison, and the average duration of prior commitments. Finally, some items related to time in prison or prison housing: weeks in prison prior to our visit, weeks spent in present housing, and time left to serve on the present sentence.

The various predictor variables are, of course, likely to be interrelated in complex ways. For this reason, the regression analyses were done in phases. First, the influence of background variables was assessed. Then we determined the additional impact of criminal history variables. Finally, the added influence of the time variables was assessed. In this way the influence of the criminal history variables cannot be attributed to major background differences, and the influence of time in prison cannot be attributed to differences in home and criminal background.

Our main interest in these analyses was to determine factors that influenced reactivity to crowded housing. The open dorms in our sample provided the best housing for this analysis, while singles would serve as the best comparison group. There were not sufficient numbers of doubles residents in our sample for the multivariate analyses. Supposedly, if a variable predicts reactivity to dorms but not to singles, we have some basis for considering this variable as a moderator of reactivity to crowding. Furthermore, the multiple regression analyses were designed to indicate which of the variables best predicted the various measures of reactivity to dormitory housing. The overall variance accounted for by the predictor variables (R^2) will provide an indication of the overall predictive utility of these variables.

Background Factors

As argued earlier, the past history of the inmate may influence his reaction to his present housing. One might expect low socioeconomic status to be related to a more positive response to prison housing because of past deprivations. Alternatively, higher socioeconomic level might be related to better coping ability and hence better adjustment. The size of either a childhood or adulthood hometown may also be relevant since growing up in crowded urban areas could influence tolerance for crowded prison living. The results for the multiple regression analyses for residents in singles and in dormitories for six background variables (entered simultaneously: occupation of parent, completion of parent's high school education, school grades completed, homesize, and size of hometown) are shown in Table 6–1. Background variables generally accounted for only a small amount of

TABLE 6–1. Influence of background variables in multiple regression analyses for singles and dorms

Criterion variable		Predictor variable	Beta	Significance	R² for all variables	N
Perceived	S	Parent's occupation[c]	.17	.05	.06	172
crowding[a]	D	Grade in school	.28	.01	.10	145
Room	S	None			.06	172
rating[b]	D	Grade in school	−.29	.001	.11	145
Systolic	S	None			.02	172
blood	D	Hometown as adult	−.21	.03	.07	159
pressure						
Diastolic	S	Hometown as adult	−.21	.01		172
blood		Parent's school	.19	.03	.10	172
pressure	D	Homesize	−.15	.06	.05	159
Mood[b]	S	None			.07	74
	D	Parent's occupation	−.31	.02	.12	80
Tense-	S	None			.05	74
stimulation[b]	D	Hometown as adult	.32	.01		
		Parent's occupation	−.28	.02	.26	80
Crowding	S	None			.06	74
complaints[a]	D	Homesize	−.39	.01		67
		Parent's school	.27	.04	.26	67
Choice[b]	S	Grade in school	−.27	.05	.10	74
	D	Grade in school	−.44	.001		81
		Hometown as child	−.23	.05	.30	81

Notes: [a] High is negative.
[b] High is positive.
[c] See Table 4–2 for values of predictor variables.

variance, but they did reveal a consistent pattern. Higher educational achievement or higher occupational and educational level of parents were related to generally negative reactions to the prison environment (perceived crowding, room rating, mood state, and crowding complaints), particularly in the case of dormitories. Larger homesize was related to lower blood pressure and fewer crowding complaints, especially in dormitories. Residence in a large hometown as an adult was related to lower blood pressure and a more positive mood state, but residence in a large town was related to less feeling of choice in dorms. The background variables also accounted for considerably more variance for the dorm residents than the single residents.

These results indicate that the education, socioeconomic, and hometown variables influence reaction to crowded housing more than they influence reaction to singles. In general, a higher education or socioeconomic level was related to negative reactions to prison living, and dormitories in particular. This may reflect the fact that prison conditions may provide a more negative contrast to prior living conditions for individuals of a somewhat higher education-socioeconomic background than for those with a poorer background. Growing up with many others in one's home or living in a large city was also related to relatively favorable reactions to dormitories. It is possible that these experiences allow one to adapt to or learn to cope with crowded living conditions to some extent (cf. Eoyang, 1974; Loo & Ong, 1984).

One other factor one might expect to be important in reactions to crowding is age. We anticipated that older inmates would be somewhat more solicitous of privacy. Our interviews often elicited complaints from older inmates about the noise made by the younger ones. Yet analyses indicated that age of the inmates does not appear to be related to differential reaction to housing. The only variable strongly affected by age was blood pressure.

Criminal History

The impact of criminal history was assessed by entering the previously discussed background factors first and then by entering the criminal history variables simultaneously. These variables were custody level, number of prior commitments to prison, and duration of prior commitments (in weeks). Custody level reflects both a between-institution and a within-institution factor. Higher levels of custody (less security) would involve more freedom, fewer restrictions, and housing with similar-custody inmates. One would expect higher custody to be related to more favorable reactions. Indeed, the analysis supports this view, with high levels of custody related to lower feelings of crowding, more positive room ratings, and lower illness rate, particularly in singles (Table 6–2). However, blood

TABLE 6–2. Contribution of criminal history variables in multiple regression analyses for singles and dorms

Criterion variable		Predictor variable	Beta	Significance	R^2 for all variables	N
Illness	S	Custody[c]	−.18	.03	.09	157
	D	None			.10	110
Perceived	S	Custody	−.18	.04	.09	157
crowding[a]	D	Custody	−.21	.05	.17	110
Room rating[b]	S	Custody	.25	.01	.14	157
	D	None			.15	110
Systolic blood	S	Custody	.16	.06	.06	157
pressure	D	None			.09	110
Diastolic blood	S	Custody	.23	.01	.20	157
pressure	D	Priors	.29	.07	.18	110

Notes: [a] High is positive.
[b] High is negative.
[c] Less restrictive custody, higher values (Table 4–2).

pressures are higher in singles with higher levels of custody, and in dorms with more prior incarcerations. Although no effects were observed for the criterion variables added later in the project (e.g., mood, control), this may be due primarily to the small sample size available for the multiple regression analyses. It might also be noted that the addition of the criminal history variables led to a reasonable increase in variance accounted for by all of the variables in most cases.

The results for custody are somewhat difficult to interpret since custody reflects both the criminal history of the inmate and institution differences. In general, less severe custody (less severe criminal history and less restrictive prison environment) is related to positive reactions. While this result fits with prior expectations, the elevated blood pressure for less secure custody inmates was unexpected. This finding cannot be attributed to possible confounding with age since the effect remains when this factor is controlled. The higher levels of activity of inmates in less secure environments may be associated with elevated blood pressures during the day. For example, in a study of jails, it was found that inmates who had just returned from work outside the institution had relatively high blood pressures (Paulus & McCain, 1983).

Custody represents in part the degree of criminal history as reflected in the other two measures—number of priors and their duration. However, to determine more directly the extent to which these might play a role in reactions to prison housing, several separate univariate analyses were done. These revealed that the duration of past confinements primarily influenced reactivity to dormitory living. Inmates who had been confined for prior crimes for 40 weeks or more rated dorms significantly more negatively (perceived crowding 3.4 versus 2.9, room rating 11.1 versus 16.2, and choice 3.8 versus 4.6) than inmates who had been incarcerated for less than 40 weeks. Although custody level with its associated freedoms may be related to positive reactions to prior housing (particularly in singles), inmates who have extensive prison experience find dormitory living rather unpleasant. It is possible that inmates who have extensive prior prison experience spent a large part of that time in nondormitory housing. Thus they may be particularly sensitive to the deprivations of dormitory housing relative to single or double cells.

Length of Confinement

Although the major focus of the project has been on the effects of crowding, some of the data is also pertinent to the issue of prison confinement. Much research has been conducted on the impact of being confined in prisons (Bukstel & Kilmann, 1980; Flanagan, 1981; McKay, Jayewardene, & Reedie, 1979). Although it is difficult to compare inmates with noninmate groups, one can examine the impact of length of confinement in prison.

Lengthy confinement in the prison may be associated with positive reactions because of increasing familiarity and feelings of control or mastery over the environment. With increased time in prison, the inmate may learn the "rules of the game" in the prison and may learn to cope with its deprivations and dangers. Another time-related factor is the amount of time the inmate expects to stay in prison. Inmates who expect to serve a long time may try to make their stay more tolerable by developing more positive attitudes toward the enviroment (cognitive reevaluation). Time in prison was measured by the recorded number of weeks in the present prison and served on the present sentence. Time left on sentence was measured by the reported months left to serve. Multiple regression analyses were done in which backgound and criminal history were entered first, and then the time variables were entered simultaneously.

Residents in singles would appear to be the best population for assessing the impact of confinement factors. These inmates have generally been confined somewhat longer than other inmates and they are not exposed to crowded housing conditions. The length of present confinement indeed seems to be a major factor for singles residents. Longer time in prison was related to greater feelings of crowding, more negative room rating, and lower feelings of choice. Longer weeks committed on present sentence were related to lower feelings of choice but also lowered systolic blood pressure. In general singles residents show increasingly negative psychological reactions with increased length of confinement in prison. However, the lower blood pressure with increased length of confinement suggests that inmates may be adapting or adjusting to their environment somewhat, even though they have increasingly negative feelings about it.

In dorms, increased time in prison was related only to increased feelings of choice, while more time committed was related to greater feelings of choice and fewer problems with headaches. More time left to serve was related to a higher illness rate, lower room rating, and more crowding complaints (Table 6–3). The addition of the time factor added only a small amount to the total variance accounted for by all variables. In general, these analyses indicate that for singles, increased time in prison was related to negative psychological reactions, but also lowered blood pressure. Longer time in dorms was related to some positive reactions, while time left to serve (and presumably less time already spent in prison) was related to negative reactions.

Summary

We have presented the results of a series of analyses designed to determine the extent to which various background or experiential factors influence appraisal of and reactions to prison housing. The analysis of background variables revealed a number of consistencies. Higher socioeconomic and

TABLE 6–3. Contribution of time factors in multiple regression analyses for singles and dorms

Criterion variables		Predictor variables	Beta	Significance	R² for all variables	N
Illness	S	None			.08	155
	D	Months left[c]	.28	.01	.09	120
Perceived	S	Weeks in Prison	.21	.01	.09	156
crowding[a]	D	None			.14	115
Room rating[b]	S	Weeks prison	−.16	.05	.16	156
	D	Months left	−.20	.05	.16	116
Systolic	S	Weeks committed	−.21	.02	.05	157
blood	D	None			.11	130
pressure						
Crowding	S	None			.20	40
complaints[a]	D	Months left	.32	.05	.33	46
Choice[b]	S	Weeks in prison	−.40	.01		
		Weeks committed	−.40	.01	.16	57
	D	Weeks in prison	.31	.03		
		Weeks committed	.29	.04	.25	59
Headaches	S	None			.14	77
	D	Weeks committed	−.53	.05	.18	31

Notes: [a] High is negative.
   [b] High is positive.
   [c] High values, more time.

education levels were related to negative reactions to prison housing in general, and to dormitories in particular. Possibly for these individuals, prison represents a greater level of deprivation or greater degree of contrast in quality between their prior environment and their current one. Individuals of lower socioeconomic or education status may have learned to tolerate and cope with personal deprivations encountered in prison (e.g., lack of privacy, poor food, poor climate control, and potential physical danger).

Growing up in a home with a large number of other people or living in a large city (over 30,000) was related to relatively lower blood pressures and somewhat more positive reactions to dorms. Apparently a history of crowding in the home or exposure to urban density may facilitate adaptation to dormitory living. These residents may have learned techniques or coping skills to make these situations tolerable (cf. Milgram, 1970). Alternatively, they may simply view dense living situations as less unpleasant because they have different reference points of what constitutes crowding compared to residents who are used to less crowded environs. The issue is discussed in detail in the next section of this chapter.

The influence of criminal history variables was also examined. Custody level, which reflects type of institution, severity of sentence, and time in prison, was related to reactivity to prison housing, particularly in singles.

Less restrictive custody was related to more positive reactions. A more direct analysis of duration of prior confinements revealed that an extensive prison history is associated with negative reactions to dormitories. Thus it appears that extensive prior prison history leads to less tolerance for crowded prison housing. One reason may be that individuals with an extensive prison history are likely to have spent part of their time in single cells, especially toward the end of their sentences. This may make them especially sensitive to the relative deprivation of living in dormitories. The impact of total length of confinement for the present prison term was also considered. The influence of this variable is more apparent in singles, perhaps because one finds a broader range of confinement time for inmates in such housing. Furthermore, in singles the effects of confinements may be seen as being independent of reactions to crowded housing. Increased length of confinement in singles was related to negative psychological reactions but also lowered blood pressure. Although some degree of physiological adjustment may occur with increased length of confinement in prison, psychological reactions to the prison environment become increasingly negative.

In general, the results of the background and experiential variables suggest that these may be important in determining reaction to crowded living conditions. One could view these variables as influencing the appraisal process in the theoretical models discussed earlier. One is likely to evaluate or appraise one's present environment in terms of one's past success in this setting, one's past exposure to similar settings (comparison level), and the degree to which one values privacy or desires social contact (social needs or tolerance). These factors influence the extent to which an environment elicits positive or negative reactions. The fact that the background variables (socioeconomic, education, homesize, and hometown) were the primary ones to predict differential reactions to dormitories suggests that these types of factors are more pertinent to reactivity to crowded living conditions than criminal history and time factors. The criminal history and time-related variables (with the exception of duration of prior confinement) predicted primarily the reaction to housing in general, or singles in particular.

Tolerance for Prison Crowding

So far we have provided evidence both for stress-related effects of dormitory housing and of the influence of various personal and experiential factors on this relationship. An underlying assumption guiding our analyses is that background factors influence the extent to which individuals can tolerate crowded conditions. Experiences that breed tolerance should presumably be related to lower levels of stress in crowded conditions. It would be of interest, however, to examine more precisely the role of tolerance in mediating reactions to crowded housing. To what extent do background factors influence tolerance of crowding? Does tolerance for crowding actually influence the extent to which crowded conditions elicit negative psychological and health-related reactions?

The specific issue of tolerance development has only seen superficial treatment in theoretical models. For example, Wohlwill and Kohn (1973) used an adaptation level model to account for reactions of migrants to Harrisburg, Pennsylvania. Those who came from a large city rated this city more favorably than those who came from a small town. Thus one's experience in a prior environment may become the criterion by which one judges subsequent environments. Past experiences in crowded and privacy-deprived environments should lead one to judge subsequent crowded environments more favorably. Yet few studies have explicitly examined tolerance, its development independent of coping responses, and subjective evaluation of the environment. Desor (1972) pioneered such an approach in the crowding area by presenting subjects with simulated rooms in which they could place small figures representing people. She varied the dimensions of these rooms and the activities that subjects were to imagine in them. This technique was used successfully by Sales, Guydosh, and Iacano (1974) to demonstrate greater tolerance for crowding among high sensation seekers. We have used this technique with moderate success to assess tolerance for crowding in prison inmates as a function of crowding in their housing.

An underlying assumption of a tolerance approach is that expressed tolerance taps directly one's sensitivity to various potentially unpleasant environmental and social conditions. In essence a measure of tolerance might provide one with a relatively direct indication of the outcome of the variety of factors discussed earlier. Thus individuals who have become less sensitive or have learned to cope successfully with crowding should evidence higher levels of tolerance. An interesting possibility is that tolerance and evaluation of environmental conditions may be relatively independent. Someone who has learned to live under deprived conditions may develop a tolerance for such conditions and show little evidence of stress. However, this same person may come to judge this environment in a negative way and be strongly motivated to attain improved living conditions. This model could be seen as a compensatory one in which individuals are strongly motivated to exceed or avoid conditions of past deprivation. One important goal of our project was to develop some relatively precise measures of tolerance and relate these to various measures of adjustment to prison housing.

Crowding Tolerance Test

In our research we have employed various techniques to assess tolerance for crowded living conditions. These techniques involved assessing the individual's subjective reaction to various housing arrangements. In our early studies we employed a figure placement task in which inmates were asked to place figures in a model of an open dormitory (Desor, 1972). They were asked to put in as many figures as they could without making it "too crowded." We found that inmates living in crowded dormitories showed less tolerance on this task than those living in less crowded housing. Furthermore, the longer they lived in the dormitories, the lower the tolerance. These results suggest that the experience of crowding may lead to increased valuation of privacy or low levels of crowding (Paulus et al., 1975). In our subsequent research we have had only mixed success with this tolerance task, and as a result we developed several other measures. One rather direct measure of tolerance involved presenting inmates with schematics of open dormitories, with bunks representing the number of inmates housed in them. There were eight schematics in which the number of bunks increased in order from 8 to 22. The drawings were shown to the inmates one at a time, and the inmate was asked to indicate when the investigator should stop in the series, because any more bunks in the dormitories would make it "too crowded." The number of bunks on the last drawing shown was presumed to reflect the individual's tolerance for dormitory living.

Inmates in dorms had significantly higher ($p < .001$) tolerance scores (12.3) than those in singles (10.9) or doubles (9.0). Furthermore, the tolerance measure appears to strongly differentiate reactions to dormitory housing, but not to singles and doubles. Higher tolerance is associated with more favorable housing ratings, fewer crowding complaints, lower perceived crowding and more positive feelings on the tense-stimulated scales in dormitories. There was also a trend for illness complaints to be lower with higher tolerance in dormitories ($p < .06$) (Table 6–4). It should

TABLE 6–4. Results for tolerance measures for dorm residents[a]

Variables	Tolerance		People	Space
	≤12	≥13		
Perceived crowding[b]	3.16	2.39	3.2	2.7
Room rating[c]	13.21	20.59		
Crowding complaints[b]	1.51	.95		
Mood[c]			18.63	21.65
Tense-stimulated[c]	6.58	9.00	7.0	8.85
Choice[c]			3.88	4.52
Illness[b]	.27	.13		
Parent's school[d]	.53	.28		
Age	32.0	28.6		
Last grade	9.6	7.9		

Notes: [a] All differences significant beyond the $p = .05$ level except for illness, $p = .06$.
[b] High scores are negative.
[c] High scores are positive.
[d] 1 = graduate, 0 = no.

be noted that mean tolerance ranged from 8 to 13 in the three housing conditions. The dormitories in the tolerance test were drawn to the scale of dormitories in one prison which each held from 26 to 40 inmates. It can also be seen in Table 6–4 that high-tolerance inmates in dorms were somewhat younger and of lower education and socioeconomic status than the low-tolerance inmates.

All inmates were also asked whether they were more bothered by having too many people or too little space in their living unit. This measure was designed to assess differential sensitivity to having to deal with people or having inadequate space. The people-space measure was also clearly related to differential reactions to dormitories. In dormitories, inmates who are bothered more by people feel more crowded, evaluate their housing more negatively, have more negative mood states, and lower feelings of choice than inmates who are bothered by too little space. No effects of this measure were obtained for singles and doubles.

The tolerance and people-space measures of crowding tolerance provide generally consistent results. Scores on these measures strongly differentiate reactions to dormitories, but were related to only a few differential reactions to singles and doubles. It may be noted that no multivariate analyses were done for the preceding tolerance measures. The number of inmates in the sample was simply too small to do an adequate analysis. However, analyses for the two measures for which the largest sample was available (perceived crowding and room rating) indicated that the influence of the tolerance measure remains even after controlling for the other predictor variables (socioeconomic, criminal, and time related).

Housing Preference Test

We also developed a housing preference test to allow a more fine-grained analysis of crowding tolerance. The two measures of tolerance discussed so far have focused primarily on general tolerance for people in housing. Even though the phrasing of the people-space question suggests that it is tapping two dimensions, the question is basically one-dimensional. In the housing preference test we tried to construct alternatives that would indicate the extent to which individuals were sensitive to the number of dorm residents, amount of space, and a rooming situation involving doubles. This preference test consisted of 23 pairs of drawings that represented two different types of prison housing. These pairs varied in the number of people depicted as living in the units and the amount of space allotted. A factor analysis indicated the existence of four subgroups of items. Each of these sets of items tapped sensitivity to social density in slightly different ways. The results of analyzing the predictive power of these four subgroups were basically similar to that of the tolerance measures previously discussed— greater tolerance for social density was related to positive reactions to dormitory living. Consequently, we will spare the reader the details (see

Paulus, 1984). However, there was some indication that those items which involved both sensitivity to the amount of space and the number of people predicted reactions to singles. Since the housing preference test was used throughout the research project, the sample size was sufficient for multivariate analyses. These indicated that a greater duration of past confinement and a shorter time in prison were related to a greater preference for low social density. However, the effects of preference were obtained even when one controlled for these and other predictor variables.

Summary

Tolerance for crowding was measured in a variety of ways, but for each of these measures, greater tolerance for crowding or people was associated with more favorable reactions to dormitories, but not to doubles or singles. The tolerance measures seem to tap quite well the sensitivity to living in crowded dorms, but not the reactivity to living in singles or doubles. These findings suggest that tolerance for crowding is not a global or general trait. Instead, tolerance for different types of housing may be rather specific to that type of housing. The results on background factors also reinforce the conclusion that only specific types of crowding experience affect reactivity to crowding in specific housing types.

Future research will have to determine more precisely the role of tolerance in reaction to crowded environments. In particular, longitudinal studies will be required to assess the causal role of tolerance. Our present results for the tolerance measures could be interpreted either as the impact of tolerance on negative reactions to housing or the impact of negative reactions to housing on tolerance for specific housing.

Conclusions

We have found that certain background factors do seem to play a role in crowding. In general, it appears that growing up under low socioeconomic conditions and in relatively crowded home environments reduces one's negative reactions. These experiences may prepare individuals for living under such conditions, or these conditions may simply be seen as relatively less unpleasant in comparison to past living conditions. However, those with extensive prior prison history did not have a reduced reactivity to crowded housing conditions. Experiences and habits formed in past incarcerations may not be pertinent or useful for dormitory living. Those with an extensive prison history may also use their past experience in singles or doubles as reference points and hence judge dormitories more negatively.

Background differences seem to influence degree of tolerance for crowded living conditions. Specific measures of the degree of crowding tolerance appear to be useful in predicting reactivity to crowding. In particular, those who indicate higher degrees of tolerance of social density evidence a lower level of negative reactions to dormitories.

What bearing does this have on the adaptation-versus-sensitization issue discussed in the beginning of the chapter? It appears that experiences which prepare one for a certain type of living situation provide a low basis of comparison which is related to apparent adaptation to crowded living conditions. Experiences connected with counterproductive styles of relating to others or with negative reference points provide a basis for an increased sensitivity or reactivity to crowding.

7
Gender and Racial/Ethnic Differences

The last chapter demonstrated that different types of background can influence reactions to crowded living conditions. On this basis, it would seem likely that other personal characteristics that are related to background differences would also be related to the differential reactions to crowding. Gender and race or ethnic group are such characteristics and these often come up in discussions of our crowding research. Since our work has focused predominantly on males, one might question whether the observed effects may be restricted to all-male environments. Living in crowded male housing environments may be much more threatening than living in crowded female housing situations. Similarly, differences in the background of racial or ethnic groups (socioeconomic, cultural, etc.) could lead to differential adjustment to crowded prison housing. We will review some of the literature pertinent to these issues and present relevant data from our prison studies.

Gender Effects

Past crowding studies have frequently examined the influence of gender; however, most of these studies were done in laboratory settings. These studies generally found that males and females react similarly to variations in social density, but males react more negatively to high spatial density than do females (cf. Paulus, 1980). Interestingly, these differences in response to spatial density were obtained only in cases where groups were all-male and all-female. These findings may reflect sex differences in personal space sensitivity. Studies on reactions to spatial invasions and preferred interpersonal distances have found that males prefer relatively larger distances from other males compared to the distances preferred by females. Preferred distances for male-female pairs appear to be intermediate (Evans & Howard, 1973). So the relatively negative reactions of all-male groups in spatially dense conditions may reflect their sensitivity to the small interpersonal distances associated with such situations.

Based on the laboratory research, one might expect males to react more negatively to living in crowded dorms than females. However, one series of studies observed no sex differences in reactions to corridor dorms relative to suite dorms (Baum & Valins, 1977), while in another study, female residents had more difficulties with the tripling of college dormitory rooms than males (Aiello et al., 1975). Tripling of rooms may, of course, be a source of a variety of interpersonal tensions unrelated to crowding, since two of the roommates may form a coalition against the remaining one (Aiello, Baum, & Gormley, 1981). One study of inmates in a prison for females found that females living in multiple-occupant rooms liked their rooms less than those living in single rooms (Ruback & Carr, 1984). These findings are similar to those obtained in our studies of male inmates.

It is difficult to make confident predictions about differences in reactions of males and females to living in prison dormitories. Compared with singles, these dorms are both socially and spatially crowded. However, since social density appears to be the major factor in the differences observed between singles and dorms, one might expect similar reactions from male and female residents. We were able to examine this possibility in one minimum security federal prison that housed both males and females in singles and dormitories. The singles were located along corridors with other singles or doubles and had 85 or 105 sq ft of space. The dorms consisted of open areas divided by cubicles. Each inmate had their own cubicle; female dorms contained 10 to 12 cubicles and male dorms had 16 to 24 cubicles. The cubicles were 5.5 ft high, provided 48 sq ft of space, and had an opening for a doorway. Therefore, the cubicles provided less privacy and living space than the single room. Over the period of 1 year, we were able to collect data from 54 males and 78 females. During the time of our study, the population of the institution varied from 596 to 653.

The evaluation by the male and female inmates of their housing was strikingly similar, with both groups rating the dorms as more crowded and less desirable than singles. However, with regard to somatic problems, only females reported more headache problems and had more clinic visits in dorms than in singles (Table 7–1). Why would we obtain similar evaluations of housing, but differences in somatic reactions? We examined the possibility that background differences could account for the observed effects. Residents of singles had been in prison longer and had less stringent custody designations. Females had a shorter history of past confinement than males. Yet controlling for these variables by analysis of covariance did not change the pattern of the findings.

If the health results reflect the impact of dormitory living on female inmates, these findings would be consistent with those of Aiello and co-workers (1975) that females may have more problems adjusting to crowded living conditions than males. We have found increased illness rates for male residents in open dorms in our other studies, but cubicles may eliminate or reduce the effect of crowding (at least in the case of one

TABLE 7–1. Results for housing and gender in a co-correctional prison

	Singles		Cubicles	
	Males	Females	Males	Females
Perceived crowding[a]	1.5	1.7	2.3	2.3
Room rating[b]	29.7	30.2	20.9	21.6
Headache problems	0	0	0	.11
Diastolic blood pressure	62.67	73.35	67.69	69.65
Sleep problems	.38	.59	.31	.63
Illness rate	.28	.25	.06	.53

Notes: [a] High is positive.
  [b] High is positive.

of the prisons examined). Thus, it may require a greater degree of crowding for males to demonstrate health-related effects. For females, the stress of living in cubicle dorms may be sufficient to cause health-related problems. Obviously, additional studies are needed to confirm and evaluate our results. At the very least, our results strongly confirm the assumption that females as well as males are susceptible to the negative effects of crowding. Apparently those characteristics that predispose females to react less negatively to temporary personal space invasions or spatial crowding in the laboratory do not enable them to adjust to long-term exposures to crowded housing. One possible reason for this is that sex differences in situations involving same-sex initial encounters may reflect the greater affiliative tendencies of females than males in those situations (Epstein & Karlin, 1975). These initial positive reactions may quickly dissolve in the course of encounters characterized by high degrees of interference, stimulation, and uncertainty.

Racial Effects

Although race would seem an important factor to consider in evaluating the effects of crowding in various settings, few studies have explicitly addressed this issue. Laboratory or field studies have generally ignored its potential role in reactions to crowding. Demographic studies of urban crowding have generally used race as an extraneous variable for which one needs to control in multivariate analyses. There are, however, a few hints about the role race may play in crowding effects.

In an archival study of young inmates in the Georgia State Prison System, the strongest reaction to crowding was observed for urban blacks, and the least for rural whites (Carr, 1980). Studies of personal space have also found evidence for ethnic and racial differences, but these appear to be related primarily to socioeconomic level (Jones & Aiello, 1973). Low

TABLE 7–2. Effects for race and housing

	Blacks			Whites		
	Singles	Doubles	Dorms	Singles	Doubles	Dorms
Perceived crowding[a]	1.83	3.30	3.45	1.95	3.23	3.26
Room rating[b]	23.61	12.57	12.13	23.40	12.82	12.06
Mood state[b]	26.02	25.00	21.59	23.30	18.46	18.48
Choice[b]	4.16	6.00	3.76	4.28	4.19	3.61
Control[b]	8.31	7.33	7.62	8.16	6.50	6.78
Headache	.40	.67	.63	.40	.52	.74
Illness rate	.23	.21	.70	.18	.18	.27
Diastolic blood pressure	60.88	55.65	60.27	62.71	61.27	64.77
Size of hometown as child[c]	1.76	1.74	1.79	1.45	1.42	1.51
Size of hometown as adult[c]	1.77	1.87	1.95	1.65	1.67	1.73
Prior incarceration	2.46	1.28	2.49	1.86	1.28	1.92

Notes: [a] A higher score is more negative.
[b] A higher score is positive.
[c] Small is 1 and large is 2.

socioeconomic level individuals seem to have smaller personal space re-
quirements than higher socioeconomic level individuals. On the basis of
these studies, one might predict that racial differences will be observed, but
when other differences in background such as urban-rural home environs
are controlled statistically, racial differences may disappear.

Since our interest is primarily in determining racial differences in reactions to crowded dormitories, we limited our analyses to inmates living in
singles, doubles, and dorms. Black and white inmates from four prisons
that contained at least two of these types of housing were used for this
analysis.

As with gender, the evaluation of housing was essentially the same for
both groups: each rated dorms and doubles more negatively than singles
(Table 7–2). Mood states and perceived control and choice also showed
a similar pattern, with blacks evidencing a generally more positive mood
state than whites. Only for illness complaints was race related to differential reactions to housing. Although blacks had generally higher illness complaint rates, this was particularly true for dormitory residents. The typical
illness effect observed in dorms appears to be stronger for blacks than for
whites. Since not all of the institutions were equally represented in the
various housing conditions, the effects obtained could be attributed in part
to this discrepancy. Therefore, similar analyses were performed for two
prisons that housed inmates in both singles and dorms. This greatly reduced our sample size, but again the effects for illness complaints were in
the same direction (this time only marginally significant).

As with gender, we have found that psychological reactions (environment rating, mood, etc.) to dorms as compared with singles and doubles were similar for blacks and whites, but that the clinic visit rates provide some evidence of differential reactivity of whites and blacks. Even though both groups rated dorms negatively, black inmates seem to be somewhat more prone to the negative effects of crowded living conditions. Of course, black and white inmates may differ along other dimensions besides race, and these differences could account for the observed racial effects. In examining racial differences in background and criminal history, two major factors were found to differentiate the two groups strongly. Blacks tended to come from towns with populations greater than 30,000, and they had a greater number of prior incarcerations. When these two factors are employed as covariates, the differential effects of race for clinic visits no longer approach significance.

Our data on gender and race did not indicate that these alone are important factors in determining the degree of reaction to crowding. Males and females and blacks and whites found dorms similarly unpleasant as compared with singles and doubles. Yet both the females and the black males in dorms showed greater elevation of rates of clinic visits than females and black males in singles and doubles. These results suggest a certain degree of independence of psychological and somatic reactions in response to crowded environments. It is possible that although all of the groups perceived dormitories in a negative fashion, these verbal measures may not fully tap the stress experienced by inmates and reflected in clinic visits. Alternatively, females and black males (given their experience) may have lower thresholds for responding to or reporting of symptoms in unpleasant environments. Precise measurement of various physiological indicators of stress would be most helpful in unraveling this puzzle.

The broad picture we have developed so far indicates that race and gender may have little bearing on subjective reactions to crowded living conditions. Racial differences that were observed for illness complaints were related to crowding-related background differences. Furthermore, gender differences in illness complaints in dorms may also be related to the fact that males had not been in prison long enough to develop substantial illness histories. Based on these results, it does not appear that reactions to crowding in natural settings are significantly influenced by gender and race, independent of crowding-related experience.

Ethnic Differences

Thus far we have restricted our analyses to individuals who, for the most part, have grown up in American society. However, in some prisons, there is a significant group of inmates who have grown up in other countries. For example, at La Tuna FCI (near the U.S.-Mexican border), we found a substantial number of inmates who were Mexican Nationals. This prison also contained large numbers of Mexican-Americans as well as the usual complement of Anglo-Americans. It seemed quite tenable to us that Mexican Nationals would find living in crowded quarters much less aversive than would the other inmates. Most residents of Mexico live in very crowded urban areas or in crowded housing with little privacy and have a very low standard of living. These factors may combine to make these residents more tolerant of living in crowded dormitories compared with residents who grew up in the United States.

In the course of several research visits, we were able to obtain data from 71 Anglo-Americans, 35 Mexican-Americans, and 51 Mexican Nationals. We equated groups for criminality by excluding Mexican Nationals that were incarcerated for individual illegal entry. We employed Spanish-speaking assistants and Spanish language forms with the Spanish-speaking inmates. Housing inside the prison consisted primarily of large, double-bunked open dormitories with 65 to 70 occupants. Space per person was approximately 30 sq ft. Outside the prison was a modern minimum security camp consisting of four wings in which inmates were housed in bays with four bunks. When occupied by four inmates, these bays provided 31 sq ft of space per person. Typically two to three inmates shared the bays. Two wings had 7 bays and the other two had 14 bays. Interestingly, we did not obtain a corridor length effect, as has been reported for college dormitories by Baum and Valins (1977).

For residents of both types of housing, Mexican Nationals responded most positively and Anglo-Americans most negatively on the majority of measures—perceived crowding, room rating, choice, control, and reported problems with sleeping (Table 7–3). These results suggest that the differences in cultural experiences of these three groups have led to considerable differences in tolerance for the deprivations of prison life and communal living. This is supported by the fact that Mexican-Americans had the greatest overall reported tolerance for crowding and Anglo-Americans the least. Furthermore, there was also evidence that these differences in sensitivity were related to the degree to which the inmates experienced stress. Anglo-Americans had the highest illness complaint rates and Mexican Nationals the lowest. Mexican Nationals also had lower diastolic blood pressures than the other groups. Although it seems reasonable to suppose that these observed differences among the ethnic groups represent differences in reaction to the prison environment, we do not have a comparison group of nonincarcerated individuals to use as a basis of comparison. Thus the reader should keep in mind that the ethnic differences observed could reflect differences in "response sets" of these ethnic groups independent of the environment.

Our main interest was to determine whether there existed ethnic differences in reaction to dormitory living when the two- to three-person bays are used as a basis of comparison. Dormitories were, in fact, associated with a variety of negative reactions relative to the bays: feelings of crowd-

TABLE 7-3. Effects of ethnic group

	Bays			Dorms		
	Anglo- American	Mexican- American	Mexican National	Anglo- American	Mexican- American	Mexican National
Perceived crowding[a]	2.7	1.9	1.2	3.4	3.1	1.7
Room rating[b]	21.60	27.59	31.0	11.53	13.64	26.21
Mood[b]	20.6	25.1	27.2	20.0	19.5	21.9
Choice[b]	3.82	4.38	6.11	3.83	4.93	6.33
Control[b]	7.27	8.77	9.11	5.75	5.07	8.22
Sleep problems[a]	.60	.59	.14	.65	.63	.52
Crowding complaints[a]	.52	.33	.05	.40	.79	.24
Tolerance	10.6	12.5	12.4	11.7	11.6	15.3
Diastolic blood pressure	68.64	62.22	59.91	63.87	68.94	61.45
Systolic blood pressure	127.20	119.78	123.55	117.13	122.12	113.72
Illness rate	.18	.20	.10	.30	.12	.12

Notes: [a] High is negative.
   [b] High is positive.

ing, negative room ratings, low levels of perceived control, negative mood, and sleeping problems. However, systolic blood pressures were higher in cubicles than in dorms (Table 7–3). However, on only three measures was there evidence of differential reactions to housing type related to ethnic group (i.e., significant statistical interactions). Mexican Nationals did not differ as strongly in their reactions to the two types of housing (room rating) as did the other groups, and diastolic blood pressure was elevated for Mexican-Americans in the dorms and for whites in the bays. There were a number of differences in background characteristics and prison experience among the ethnic groups (prison history, education level of parents, time in housing, prior incarcerations, and age). When these were controlled by analysis of covariance, only the blood pressure effect was still significant.

Although ethnic group apparently had a strong effect on overall reactions to prison life, it was related to differential reactivity to crowded dormitory housing relative to bay housing on only a few measures. Each group was fairly similar in their degree of aversion to open dorms, but as with the prior findings on gender and race, there was a difference in the degree to which housing affected somatic reactions. Only Mexican-Americans had elevated diastolic blood pressures in dorms.

Summary

What can we conclude from these studies on gender, race, and ethnic groups? First, only ethnic group was related to overall differences in evaluation of prison housing in general or dormitories in particular. Males and females and blacks and whites were very similar in their reactions to housing (with the exception of illness). When the background differences related to gender, race, and ethnic group were examined, it was evident that the ethnic groups differed most in criminal and family background. The males and females and black and white males may have been too similar in background and experience for strong differences in reactions to housing to be evident. They were similar in economical, educational, and several crowding-related experiences (e.g., sharing a bedroom while growing up). Prisons, by their very nature, tend to draw individuals primarily from the lower end of the socioeconomic spectrum, and this may account for the observed homogeneity in background and for the lack of differences in housing reactions. That strong effects were obtained for the three ethnic groups may reside in the fact that these groups did indeed have rather different backgrounds.

A generally consistent picture emerges from the data presented in this chapter. An individual's gender, race, and ethnic group do not strongly influence evaluation of crowded housing compared with uncrowded housing. Strong cultural differences are associated with differences in reactions to prison housing in general. Gender, race, and ethnic group were related to differences in illness complaint rates or blood pressure in crowded housing. In the case of race, we were able to account for this effect in terms of crowding-related experience. This result was nicely consistent with that of the chapter on background differences. It is possible that more detailed information on prior crowding-related experiences would have allowed us to account for the gender and ethnic differences as well. However, susceptibility to physiological debilitation in response to stressful environments may not be fully revealed by the verbal reports of psychological reactions. Verbal reports may be tied more strongly to objective features of the environment (space, population, programs, etc.) than somatic reactions. Illness complaints and other physiological measures may be related to differences in the extent to which the environment is actually experienced as stressful.

8
Theoretical Implications

A wide variety of results on prison crowding has been presented. In various places, the theoretical meaning of some of the results has been discussed, but so far no attempt has been made to provide a broad theoretical perspective for the range of these findings. There were few theoretical models available when we began our research, but this gap was quickly filled with a wide array of alternatives. Most of these perspectives were quite limited in scope and did not have the benefit of explicit tests of the hypothesized processes. They will not be examined in detail here, since this has been done elsewhere (see Baum & Paulus, 1987). In this chapter, the major elements emphasized by these models will be outlined and a theoretical model designed to account for the broad pattern of results will be presented.

Theoretical Analyses of Crowding

One of the first theoretical perspectives to gain popularity focused on the degree to which the stimulation produced by crowded situations overloaded the mental capacities of the individual (cf. Milgram, 1970). This stimulus or information overload was presumed to have a wide variety of negative effects—decrements in task performance, negative affect, and social withdrawal. These effects could carry over into other situations even after the person left the crowded environment. Another popular perspective emphasized the fact that crowded situations interfere with or limit the person's ability to enact various desired tasks or behaviors (e.g., Stokols, 1976). This interference might be associated with strong emotional reactions and attempts to overcome these problems.

In an attempt to integrate the crowding literature with related literature on other stressors, various researchers proposed a model based on feelings of psychological control (e.g., Baron & Rodin, 1978). Crowded situations are seen as threatening one's ability to control one's interactions with others and one's environment. This loss of control is presumed to be

SOCIAL INTERACTION–DEMAND MODEL

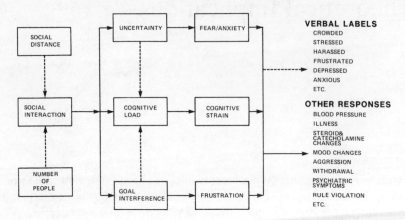

FIGURE 8–1. Social interaction–demand model (from Cox et al., 1984).

associated with feelings of helplessness, negative affect, decrements in task performance, and deterioration of health.

Although each of these mod   points to important aspects of crowded situations, these and other mo….is appear inadequate for dealing with the broad range of findings in regard to crowding. Furthermore, these models are often vague as to the critical antecedents and consequences of various crowding effects. We developed a model that incorporated the major elements of crowding emphasized by previous theoretical models, but also related these elements in such a way that a greater degree of theoretical precision is achieved (Cox et al., 1984). This model was labeled as a social interaction–demand model (Fig. 8–1), and was designed to be applicable to crowding research involving both humans and animals. Our basic assumption was that crowding has its primary impact through its influence on social interaction. Whether crowding is achieved by increasing the number of people, reducing interpersonal distance, reducing spaciousness, etc., it is the extent to which these dimensions of density influence the nature of social interaction that is important. The three aspects of social interaction that are seen as the most related to the experience of crowding and its negative effects are uncertainty, cognitive load, and goal interference.

Interactions with others generally have an element of uncertainty or unpredictability. Particularly with strangers, one can never be sure what will happen from one moment to another or what reactions will be elicited by one's own behaviors. An increase in the number of people in one's environment, their newness, and their unpredictability should increase the levels of uncertainty experienced. High levels of uncertainty will most likely produce fear or anxiety, and fear or anxiety should be greatest when the potential consequences in the situation can be relatively serious (e.g., potential physical harm).

Goal interference is frequently encountered in crowded situations. Others may hinder or delay one's carrying out of desired activities, restrict one's freedom or desire for privacy, and expose one to a variety of unwanted intrusions or distractions. When such interference becomes significant or begins affecting the achievement of highly valued goals, the individual may experience strong feelings of frustration. This frustration could lead to attempts to rectify the situation in socially acceptable ways or to angry or hostile reactions.

Crowded settings have many varied stimulation values. There may be much activity, noise, interactions, violations of personal space, etc. The cognitive strain of having to contend with all of these stimulus elements may in itself be a formidable demand on the individual's physical and psychological resources. It may lead to states such as depression or malaise, social withdrawal, and deterioration of cognitive functioning.

Thus it is proposed that social interactions in a crowded situation can, through the elements of uncertainty, interference, and cognitive load, have dramatic effects on the emotional, physical, and behavioral functioning of the individual. The psychological states produced by uncertainty, interference, and cognitive load are seen as somewhat unique, and it is likely that these states are associated primarily with certain other consequences. For example, goal interference and consequent frustration may lead to anger and violence. It is also likely that certain aspects of crowded environments influence one of the major components of interaction more strongly. For example, changes in population or turnover should primarily affect uncertainty. However, the emotional consequences of uncertainty, interference, and cognitive load are presumed to contribute jointly to overall psychological, physical, and behavioral changes. One important distinction made by the model is that verbal labels attached to the experience of crowding may or may not be consistent with various behavioral or physiological effects. Verbal labels for one's crowding experiences or status may depend on variables unrelated to density, or they may be more responsive to some aspects of density than others.

Evidential Support for the Social Interaction–Demand Model

The social interaction–demand model is responsive to a number of features of our prison data. The emphasis on social interaction reflects our findings that the number of people is more important than the amount of space. The strong impact of cubicles also suggests that the ability to control interactions is an important factor. It is more difficult to pinpoint the specific role of uncertainty, interference, and cognitive load in the effects observed. These elements were derived on the basis of our observations and analyses, but our prison research was not designed to differentiate among them. Yet some aspects of our data, as well as informal observations, support the utility of these distinctions.

The impact of turnover observed in one of our studies (McCain, Cox, Paulus, & Karlovac, 1981) probably reflects the role of the increased uncertainty of living with new arrivals. The positive effects of increased time in one's housing unit on illness rates may also be related to increased familiarity with the residents in the units (reduced uncertainty). The effects of cubicles in dormitories and of segmented dormitories may reflect primarily the reduced stimulation of unwanted intrusions from others (cognitive load).

It is likely that the main thrust of our findings on the effects of prison housing reflects the influence of all three variables. In large, crowded prisons, residents are confronted with a large number of strangers and a constant flow of new arrivals (high uncertainty). Just the sheer pressure of the large number of inmates in all segments of the prison may tax one psychologically and physically (cognitive load). The various facilities of the prison are likely to be tapped beyond capacity, leading to limited or delayed access to various services, desired activities, or private areas (interference). As a result, large crowded prisons should be associated with high levels of frustration, fear-anxiety, and cognitive strain. From this perspective, it is not surprising that such institutions are associated with high levels of pathology.

A similar case can be made for dormitories. Here the inmate may be confronted with a relatively large number of fellow residents, many of whom may be new arrivals. Relationships in such an environment involve a high amount of uncertainty. In fact, in several cases where we made informal visits with inmates who were assigned to dormitories that contained only long-termers with good behavior records, little negative reaction was elicited. This type of assignment procedure eliminates much of the uncertainty or fearful unpredictability. In crowded open dorms inmates also have many intrusions on their privacy, are often exposed to unwanted interruptions or noises, and may encounter more difficulty in the use of the sanitary or lounge facilities (interference). The activity and noise level of such dorms may contribute to cognitive load. The positive impact of cubicles in dorms may lie in their ability to reduce the cognitive load of crowding-related stimulation and the degree of uncertainty and interference experienced. An inmate living in a cubicle should have fewer unwanted encounters with other residents, be shielded somewhat from the noises and other sources of crowding-related stimulation, and experience less interference in personal activities. Since it is likely that some reasonable level of uncertainty and interference may still exist in large cubicle dormitories, one would expect that this type of housing may not aways be reacted to as positively as single rooms (as found in several studies). Uncertainty is probably not a steadily increasing function of social density in a dorm. In very large dorms, social interaction may be more intense primarily in the immediate area than in distant areas. Thus the effects might well be similar in 60- and 100-man dorms if the levels of goal interference were equalized.

So far the focus has been on the relationship of the social interaction–demand model with major crowding-related findings. Yet, a more fine-grained analysis'of the results for prison housing reveals some interesting results that also need to be accommodated by this model. For example, the discussion of the findings for singles, doubles, and dorms has focused mostly on the negative reactions to dorms. Yet, careful inspection of the results in Table 4–8 reveals an interesting pattern of results. For evaluative reactions (perceived crowding, room rating, mood state, and perceived control), doubles and dorms are rated in similarly negative terms. However, singles and doubles are similar in illness rate and headache problems, in contrast to the elevated incidence in dormitories. Although doubles and dorms produce similarly negative evaluative reactions, only dorms elicit negative somatic reactions. The results from the Danbury urine chemistry study lead to similar conclusions. While ratings of crowding increased from singles to cubicles to dorms, urine chemistry indices were elevated only in dormitories. These results are certainly contrary to a simplistic perspective that negative effects of high density are mediated by negative crowding-related feelings (cf. Stokols, 1972). This position has wide acceptance in the field, even though several scholars have taken exception to this point of view (e.g., Freedman, 1975; Paulus, 1980).

Further evidence for the importance of differentiating between evaluative and somatic reactions comes from the analysis of the impact of time in housing (see Chapter 4). Increased time in a housing unit is strongly related to a reduction in illness rates, especially in dorms. Yet, evaluative reactions (perceived crowding, room rating, and mood state) do not vary significantly over time in any of the housing conditions. This is somewhat surprising since it would seem reasonable to expect individuals either to adapt to their living conditions and become more favorable or, in the case of dormitories, become increasingly more negative about living in crowded conditions. Reactions on one psychological scale, however, do change over time. Perceived control increases over time in housing for dorms but not singles.

In accordance with the overall data on housing type, the data on time in housing suggest the need to differentiate between somatic reactions, feelings of control, and other evaluative responses involving perceived crowding, mood, and ratings of the environment. The social interaction–demand model allows for such disassociations, but does not provide an explanation for them. However, a careful analysis of the density-related findings for doubles and dormitories suggests a possible explanation for the different patterns of results for illness complaints and feelings of control as compared with ratings of perceived crowding, mood, and environment. Certainly, both dorms and doubles provide for higher levels of potential interference than singles. Because of the confined space in doubles, interference may be fairly similar in both doubles and dorms. The doubles in our studies mostly ranged between 45 and 54 sq ft in the amount of floor space. When one deducts for bunks, sanitary facilities, clothes storage, and other amenities, there is about 10 sq ft of clear space per inmate. Getting up, dressing, and most other activities require a good deal of coordination and inevitably result in substantial interference. The dormitories investigated had a range of 34 to 68 sq ft per inmate, and the population ranged from 21 to 76 inmates. There are a variety of sources of interference in dorms. One of the most obvious is noise, which can make sleeping, studying, or reading quite difficult. Another source of interference can be the number of available facilities. In one dorm, there were bunks for 86 individuals, but only two urinal troughs. Finally, in dorms, there are generally a number of inmates in the aisles, creating difficulties in simply moving from one area to another.

The degree of social stimulation may also be fairly similar for both doubles and dorms. In dorms, one is exposed to many people in an open area, and in doubles, one is exposed to potentially intense contact within one's room in addition to the casual contact in the hallways. These two relatively salient environmental conditions (interference and cognitive load) should not change much over time and may be the primary basis for ratings of the environment. This would explain both the similarity in the ratings of doubles and dorms and the lack of change in these ratings over time.

Uncertainty represents, to a large degree, the unpredictability and lack of familiarity with others in an environment. Although these factors are present in all prison housing environments, they are more likely to be a problem in open dorms. In open dorms, one potentially has to deal with a large number of co-residents without the control or regulatory mechanisms provided by rooms or privacy cubicles. Having one's own room or sharing it with only one person greatly reduces the extent to which one is unwillingly exposed to a whole range of unpredictable encounters with other residents and increases the extent that one can limit unwanted interactions. Also, in the case of the institutions we studied, dormitories often represented the initial housing assignment for inmates. Consequently, dormitories typically have more instances of turnover in residents than do units composed of singles or doubles. One consequence of the high turnover rate is the continual presence of many strangers, a factor which should contribute to the degree of uncertainty experienced by the resident (cf. McCain et al., 1981). This reasoning suggests that the effects of dormitory crowding on somatic reactions and feelings of control may lie in the degree of uncertainty that characterizes this environment, while the nega-

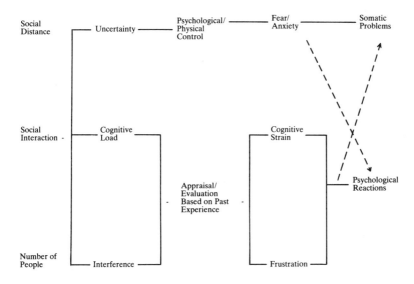

FIGURE 8–2. A revised social interaction–demand model.

tive psychological reactions to doubles and dorms are more related to the degree of social stimulation and interference (see Fig. 8–2).

The hypothesis that uncertainty is a source of somatic problems is consistent with other research showing that conditions that lead to reports of lack of control (or in our view, uncertainty) are related to physiological or health-related reactions (e.g., Mason, 1975; Folkman, 1984; Cohen et al., 1979). This research suggests that environmental, social, or personal factors that reduce uncertainty also can reduce the health-related stress reactions. Research by Ruback and colleagues (Ruback & Carr, 1984; Ruback et al., 1986) provides additional support for the role of perceived control in reactions to prison housing.

The social interaction–demand model is also relevant to the results of a large number of analyses designed to assess the background or experiential factors that influence appraisal of and reactions to prison housing. In general, the results of the background and experiential variables suggest that these may be important in determining reactions to crowded living conditions. One is likely to evaluate or appraise one's present environment in terms of one's past success in this setting, one's past exposure to similar settings, and how much one values privacy or desires social contact. These factors influence the extent to which an environment elicits positive or negative reactions. Furthermore, past success in a particular environment may also influence feelings of control and somatic reactions. It should be noted that only a small amount of the illness variance is accounted for by the background or experiential factors (about 3% or less in the overall analysis). In contrast, a much larger percentage of the variance of psychological reactions is accounted for by these same variables (up to 20%). This finding suggests that appraisal relative to past experience affects primarily psychological reactions.

The Special Case of Violence

We have reported a number of findings that indicate that increased crowding may be related to increased disciplinary problems or violence. Our own results in this area are rather meager, however, and there exists considerable controversy over the often-presumed link between crowding and violence (e.g., Ellis, 1984; Ekland-Olson, 1986). In reviewing the research on crowding and prison violence, Ellis (1984) suggests that changes in social density may be related to changes in age composition, transiency, scarcity of and competition for resources, and changes in the social control processes in the prison. Hence, any relationship of crowding to violence needs to be examined for the potential role of these factors. Ekland-Olson (1986) proposes that violence in prison is related to attempts by inmates to attain control over their life in prison. Inmates may respond with violence to their lack of control and the uncertainty produced by such factors as inmate turnover, staff changes, and court orders. On the basis of data from the Texas prison system, Ekland-Olson argues that density has little independent influence on the occurrence of violence. This conclusion is based on only one set of data and is subject to alternative evaluations (see Chapter 3). However, Ekland-Olson's (1986) proposal that social control processes underlie much of the prison violence seems to have some merit and deserves further study. The views of Ellis and Ekland-Olson are not necessarily inconsistent with the social interaction–demand view that emphasizes the role of variables related to changes in social density (interference, uncertainty, and cognitive load). Any variables in addition to social density that influence the degree of interference, uncertainty, and cognitive load are likely to have an influence on the degree of stress experienced in prison. Ellis (1984) and Ekland-Olson (1986) have provided an important service by clearly outlining the complex interaction of social density, age, resources, transiency, and social control and their potential relationship to violence in prisons. An investigation of the relationship between density and prison violence needs to be attuned to these issues as well as to the various pertinent methodological and statistical problems.

To provide a clearer conceptual basis for the evaluation of the implications of the present research on crowding and violence in prisons, we will briefly evaluate this issue from the vantage point of the general literature on violence and aggression. The literature indicates that this type of behavior is an outcome of a complex set of factors, any one of which may not be sufficient by itself as a cause. Aggressive or violent behavior is facilitated by learned propensities toward violence, events, or stimuli that serve as cues for aggressive behavior, and emotional states that enhance the probability that the aggressive inclinations will become overt (cf. Baron, 1977; Zillman, 1979). Without the existence of aggressive propensities or the occurrence of aggression-related cues, violent behavior is unlikely. When individuals with tendencies toward violence encounter aggressive stimuli (e.g., insults, purposive interference, threats), they are likely to exhibit a strong tendency toward violence. However, whether this tendency becomes an overt act depends on a variety of facilitative or inhibitive factors. Fear of punishment or retribution and social or personal norms or pressures to refrain from violent behavior may hinder the expression of violent impulses. On the other hand, social norms and support for violent behavior and a high level of arousal (whether this is a result of anger or some other source) may facilitate the expression of aggressive behavior.

On the basis of these analyses, it is not difficult to understand the occurrence of violence within prisons. Prisons often contain many violence-prone individuals who have history of involvement in violent encounters. As a part of the pressures to assert their status or toughness, inmates often exhibit a variety of behaviors that could be seen as potential aggression-eliciting stimuli (e.g., racial or personal insults, threats, verbal and physical intimidation). Furthermore, personal and social norms among inmates often favor violent solutions to interpersonal problems.

How does crowding fit into this picture? To the degree that crowding increases the occurrence of emotional states of anxiety, arousal, and fear, it may serve to enhance the probability that violence, produced by a combination of personal and social factors, becomes overt. In this light, it is interesting to note that the crowding–violence link seems stronger among relatively young inmates who are presumably more volatile than older inmates. Also as high density conditions increase the number of potential negative encounters and opportunities for personal interference, the number of potentially violent incidents may increase at a rate greater than the rate of increase in density.

Yet not all manners of increases in density should be related to increased violence. If increases in the numbers of inmates or reductions in space are accomplished without greatly increasing the interference, cognitive load, and uncertainty experienced, a crowding–violence link is unlikely to be observed. Accordingly, it is predicted that a crowding–violence relationship is most likely to occur with young violent inmates under conditions of high social density that involve high levels of unpredictable and unwanted interactions with other inmates. If there is a high degree of inmate turnover, a minimum of inmate organization or stabilization of prison life, and poor staff control in the prison, inmate violence is likely to be at a high level (Ellis, 1984; Ekland-Olson, 1986). Although density may further exacerbate these conditions, these factors could also overwhelm the more subtle influence of density (Ekland-Olson, 1986). Obviously, much research is required to document those conditions under which density is most likely to have a strong relationship to violence in prisons. Under some conditions, density may in fact be related to reduced violence. If crowding produces a high level of discomfort, residents may be more concerned with minimizing this discomfort (by seeking privacy or by social withdrawal) than with becoming more involved in intense aggressive interactions with others. In fact, some data suggest that aggressive tendencies should be greatest at moderate levels of crowding (Matthews et al., 1979). This may be particularly true if such aggressive behavior is seen as a means of achieving privacy or control over one's interactions with others.

Research designed to test the crowding–violence link is wrought with potential problems. It is difficult to obtain accurate and precise measures of institutional crowding, particularly the degree of crowding in the different housing units in the institutions. Measures of disciplinary incidents (particularly inmate-on-inmate assaults) are very indirect and may be under-reported (Ellis, 1984). Reports of violent incidents may reflect the biases of formal/informal policies of the prison staff. These may change as the degree of crowding changes. Future studies should attempt to obtain more precise and direct measures of the actual density experienced by the inmates and the reported and unreported level of violence in various housing units and prisons. Finally, measures of inmate population changes or turnover, inmate background or history of violence, staff-inmate ratio, criteria used by staff in reporting incidents, and other factors that could influence the actual or reported level of violence should be obtained.

Divergent Views

Our work has not been without its critics, who have generally emphasized the limitations of our data. For example, Bonta (1986) has argued that the relationship between prison crowding, maladaptive behavior, and health is not as clear as implied by some of our papers. He points out that the relationship between population density and violence has not been clearly established and that most of the studies are of a correlational nature. He proposes that factors such as age, length of exposure, and turnover may be important moderators of the effects of prison crowding. His points are well-taken, but certainly not inconsistent with our analysis (cf. Cox, Paulus, & McCain, 1986). For example, as pointed out in the previous section, prison violence is not seen to be an inevitable consequence of crowding. The initial propensities of the population toward violence, the quality of inmate-staff relations, and age distribution of the population are likely to be important factors. Under extremely crowded living conditions, social withdrawal may be predominant over aggressive behavior. Admittedly, the correlational nature of much of the research leaves open the possibility that variables other than crowding may have been responsible for these findings. Yet in cases where we and others were able to control for many of these alternative variables, the independent effects of density remain evident (e.g., Gaes & McGuire, 1985). Furthermore, studies in which the same individuals were shifted from one type of housing to another obtained results consistent with ours (D'Atri et al., 1981; Wener & Keys, 1986). At various places in this book, we have discussed the role of such variables as length of time spent in prison and turnover in crowding experience. They appear to influence reactions to crowding, but not necessarily in the way suggested by Bonta. While turnover does appear to enhance the negative effects of crowded living conditions, increased time in a prison environment may lead to some degree of adaptation or adjustment rather than to more severe reactions.

In an extensive review and analysis of the prison crowding literature, Gaes (1985) concluded that "research on prison crowding has not, however, convincingly demonstrated many adverse effects of crowding" (p. 95). The tentativeness of his conclusion was based on the fact that much of the evidence is rather "indirect" (e.g., verbal reports, illness complaints, and archival data). He also argued that work on crowding with animals and humans in nonprison settings was not very pertinent to the prison crowding issue. The limitations of our various findings have been candidly acknowledged throughout this volume and need not be reiterated here. However, it is felt that the overall picture is clearer and stronger than the one suggested by Gaes.

First, there is a resounding consistency in our data and of our data with the findings of other researchers. Even though each data set has its limitations, the consistency of the results from many different sources is impressive. Furthermore, our studies on individual inmates have a number of features not characteristic of most studies. We examined inmates in a wide variety of prisons and jails, and included examples of practically every type of housing found in these institutions. In selecting our sites, we focused on those institutions where questions about the impact of housing could be meaningfully assessed. There had to be a range of housing within the same institution and no major differences in the types of inmates found in these different types of housing. We used a broad range of measures (psychological, physiological, and health-related), and obtained extensive background information. In regard to our archival data, we tried to assess the adequacy of recordkeeping and the peculiarities related to institutions or changes in populations over time. We felt that it was important to carefully assess the quality of each set of information about a system. Many archival studies have simply aggregated data across systems without first going through this quality control process. The inconsistency of our results with those of others may lie in this difference in approach. Moreover, many carefully executed studies have obtained results consistent with ours.

In spite of the problems and limitations of our data and the empirical gaps that still exist, we have come a long way in our understanding of the prison crowding problem from a psychological point of view. When we began our work in 1971, the state of knowledge about prison crowding was practically zero. From that vantage point, our present state of knowledge is considerable. Now we know that the influence of space is rather minimal when compared with the influence of the number of people in one's living quarters. Open dormitories with large numbers of inmates in double bunks are a particular source of problems. Mere provision of privacy cubicles can be helpful in reducing these problems. Increasing population in prisons without commensurate increases in facilities is associated with a variety of problems indicative of deterioration of mental and physical health. Large institutions also evidence some higher levels of health-related problems. We have gained considerable insight about the influence of personal characteristics.

Much other research, both with humans and animals in the laboratory and in a variety of real-world settings, has produced results consistent with our prison data and the theoretical conclusions derived from this data. Although Gaes (1985) has minimized the importance of this literature for the understanding of prison crowding, prison crowding research should not be isolated from other research on crowding. Prison crowding research adds an important dimension to the overall crowding literature and, in the same vein, the rest of the crowding literature is pertinent for understanding the nature of prison crowding phenomena. In particular, a detailed assessment of our findings and that of others has allowed us to make considerable progress in developing a comprehensive model of crowding phenomena. This model may be of use not only in suggesting directions for further research, but also in guiding correction officials in dealing with the problems of crowding in their institutions.

Although much progress has been made, we do agree with Gaes that much additional research is warranted. Unfortunately, there appear few systematic efforts in this direction at the present time. Research in prisons is difficult, expensive, and time-consuming. It requires considerable funds and cooperative prisons, both of which are in short supply. In Chapter 9, some of the issues that remain to be addressed are outlined.

9
Practical Implications and Future Directions

In the preceding chapters, we summarized the state of knowledge in regard to crowding in general and prison crowding in particular. This chapter will provide a brief summary of the major results of our research program, outline the practical implications of these findings, and point out a variety of issues that still need to be resolved.

Major Findings

1. Changes in population in prisons are associated with changes in death rates, psychiatric commitments, suicides, and disciplinary infractions.

2. In one prison system, large institutions (>1,200) had higher death rates and psychiatric commitment rates than smaller ones (<1,200).

3. Open dormitories housing about 30 or more inmates are associated with negative evaluations and increased illness complaint rates. The strongest differences in complaints tend to be for those that are potentially verifiable or pain-related.

4. Doubles are associated with negative evaluations but not an increased rate of illness complaints.

5. The amount of space in dormitories, multiple-occupant housing, and singles does not appear to be a strong factor in predicting reactions to housing. However, there is some suggestion in our data that when inmates are confined for a large part of the day, very low levels of space can be associated with health-related reactions such as high blood pressure.

6. Privacy cubicles that provide partitions or walls around one's sleeping area appear to be quite beneficial in reducing negative reactions to open dormitory living, but may not necessarily reduce illness complaint rates.

7. Increased numbers of inmates in multiple-occupant cells are associated with increased negative reactions and illness complaints.

8. Studies of jails indicate that the number of inmates in a housing unit is more important than the amount of space; this is consistent with the finding for prisons.

9. A variety of background characteristics appear to be related to reactions to crowded housing. Relatively negative reactions to dormitories are associated with a high socioeconomic or educational level, a small hometown or small homesize, and a less extensive incarceration history.

10. The background variables appear to reflect in part a differential tolerance for living in crowded conditions. Several direct measures of crowding tolerance indicate that individuals with high degrees of expressed tolerance for crowding react less negatively to dormitories.

11. Gender, race group, and ethnic group do not appear to be important in differential reactions to crowded living conditions (singles versus dorms), independent of background differences.

12. Increased length of confinement in a particular housing unit is associated with a reduction in illness complaint rates, but housing evaluation does not change with time in housing unit.

Practical Implications

The findings presented in this volume have a number of implications for prison design standards. Some of the main ones will be briefly outlined.

1. When prisons increase in population and/or exceed designed capacity, a variety of negative effects ensue. This suggests that it is important to maintain population at moderate levels or in line with design capacity.

2. Smaller prisons appear to be desirable since they are associated with fewer health-related problems. In particular, prisons with 500 or fewer inmates evidence much fewer problems than larger ones. However, our data on prison size are not as strong as they are in relation to the degree of crowding (see also Farrington & Nuttall, 1980).

3. The impact of prison size and the degree of crowding will depend on a variety of factors such as inmate characteristics, inmate-staff relations, design of the housing quarters, inmate programming, and policies that influence inmate movement and interaction. Even a relatively crowded prison may be tolerable if it has a number of positive features (e.g., a minimum security population, a large amount of inmate programming, and the availability of privacy in housing).

The social interaction–demand model would suggest that the impact of the size or degree of crowding will depend on the extent of their relationship with the degree of uncertainty, interference, and cognitive load. A large prison with a fairly stable population (both in numbers and proneness to violent or disruptive behavior), ample facilities, and distinct subunits isolated from one another may not be a significant source of problems compared with a small prison. Inmates in such a large prison may experience a level of uncertainty, interference, and social stimulation similar to that encountered in small prisons. Perhaps the most straightforward way to achieve tolerable levels of uncertainty, interference, and social stimulation is to build small prisons. Yet it may also be possible to achieve such tolerable levels in large prisons if one controls features that influence these factors. One should probably reserve large prisons for inmates who are less likely to be a problem for others and the staff (e.g., nonviolent inmates or first offenders). Dividing a prison into distinct subunits or small prisons would help control the uncertainty and overstimulation problems. Staggering work, recreation, and eating times may diminish problems related to goal interference.

4. Double cells do not appear to be a major problem. If inmates are housed with compatible cellmates, reactions are likely to be less negative.

5. The amount of space in a housing unit within the ranges encountered in our study does not appear to be a strong factor in influencing psychological and health-related reactions. However, when inmates are confined in multiple-occupant cells with 20 sq ft or less of space per inmate, health-related reactions may ensue. Certainly the space standards of the American Correctional Association (1981) appear to be quite reasonable (60 or 70 sq ft per inmate if confined for more than 10 hours a day).

6. Limiting turnover in housing units as much as possible will help minimize some of the problems of living in crowded housing.

7. Some inmates express a high degree of tolerance for crowding and evidence a significantly lower level of crowding-related effects. With further refinement and validation, a crowding tolerance measure may be helpful to prison administrators in assigning inmates to housing. Background characteristics such as prior confinement history could also be taken into account.

Future Directions

Our program of research on crowding in prisons has yielded a large body of data and suggested the development of a theoretical model of crowding phenomena. Our knowledge and understanding of prison crowding have greatly increased. However, many empirical questions remain, and the social interaction–demand model needs explicit tests of its various assumptions and predictions. Some of the gaps that remain will be briefly addressed.

1. Most of our research on individual inmates has been in federal prisons. The conditions in these prisons are often much more benign than in state prisons and jails. It is necessary to examine a broad variety of housing in state prisons and jails to see if the same findings occur in such institutions. Is the impact of dormitory crowding the same or greater? Do

cubicles also have a beneficial effect in such environments? Will background factors such as socioeconomic level and past crowding experience moderate the effects of crowded housing? Some might argue that the effects of crowded housing in state prisons and jails will be more severe because of a greater amount of confinement in housing and the higher percentage of violent offenders. On the other hand, given that most of the inmates in these facilities have a low socioeconomic background, they may have a relatively greater tolerance for crowding than their federal prison ccunterparts.

2. The impact of the extent of daily confinement to housing needs to be examined directly. Some of our jail and prison data suggest that effects of crowded housing may be more severe when inmates are confined for large parts of the day to their housing. Confinement to single cells is a different issue, of course. This involves isolation and deprivation of physical exercise. Although these factors may be detrimental to the physical and mental health of inmates in highly crowded prisons, some inmates prefer isolation to living in crowded housing or being out in the crowded public spaces.

3. Studies need to continue to evaluate the impact of a broad variety of housing situations. The impact of the amount of space and double-bunking in dormitories and multiple-occupant cells remains to be clarified. Although space appears to be less important than initially expected, providing the inmates in dorms or multiple-occupant housing with their own bunks and adequate space for movement and possessions may yield fairly positive reactions. We have found very few such housing situations, but in one spacious single-bunk dormitory we found inmates to be quite satisfied with their housing.

4. Adjustment to living in doubles should also be studied in greater detail. Residents of doubles rated their housing about as crowded as open dorms, but did not evidence increased illness rates. What is the basis for this finding? Is it because of the increased predictability and familiarity of a one-on-one situation? If one were to change cellmates frequently, would one observe increased illness ratcs? The degree of confinement may also be important here. In federal prisons, inmates are confined to their quarters primarily at night. In cases where inmates are housed in cells most of the day, doubles may be associated with elevated stress levels because of the inevitable interference and conflicts experienced. Yet even in this situation, some inmates may prefer having a compatible cellmate to the loneliness and isolation of a single cell. Systematic studies of the impact of the degree of daily confinement across housing types are needed to illuminate these issues.

5. Although space has been shown to be of secondary importance in reactions to housing, this does not mean that it may not be an important factor under some conditions. In our study of Stateville Prison and the Houston County Jail, we found some suggestive evidence that conditions of limited space may be associated with increases in blood pressure when inmates are confined for large parts of the day. As with doubles, spatial

constriction in multiple-occupant cells may be problematic primarily if one is not given access to other spaces for one's activities; that is, the negative influence of spatial constriction may not be strongly evident unless it begins to interfere with ongoing activities and the achievement of various needs (e.g., privacy) or goals. This may not occur unless spatial density reaches very high levels (e.g., 20 sq ft per person) and/or inmates are confined to their housing for extensive periods of time.

6. One of the more interesting findings is that cubicles may reduce some of the negative impact of living in open dormitories. What is it about these cubicles that is responsible for this reduction—is it the provision of separate territories, visual isolation, interaction regulation, or sense of privacy? Studies on different arrangements and types of cubicles might help to resolve some of these questions. For example, if regulation of interaction is important, the provision of doors or gates should have a positive effect. In this regard, we have noted that the female inmates in the cubicle dorms of Fort Worth FCI often placed towels or blankets over the entrance of their cubicles.

7. The impact of the number of inmates in dorms is also unclear. In our federal prison studies, we found no difference between dorms housing 30 and 40 inmates. The reactions of residents of large dorms with 65 or more inmates were similar (in terms of perceived crowding and illness complaint rates compared with less crowded housing) to those with 30 to 40 residents in another prison. Does this mean that once one reaches some level of social density in dorms, additional residents will not have much more impact? It is possible that adding residents will increase negative reactions primarily because there is an increase in uncertainty, interference, and cognitive load. For example, if turnover levels and demand for facilities are comparable in two dorms differing in social density, there may not be much difference in inmate reactions. However, if increased social density is associated with increased turnover, greater demand on facilities, more double-bunking, and higher levels of noise and general activity, strong differences between low and high social density dorms may be observed.

8. Although we have obtained much archival data on the impact of changes in prison population and prison size, definitive data on the influence of these crowding variables require direct assessment of the health of inmates. In the case of changes in population, longitudinal studies in which inmates are monitored for physiological reactions related to changes in population would be particularly useful.

9. The focus of this volume has been on the influence of crowding variables, but many other social, environmental, and procedural factors may influence the extent to which crowding effects are observed. Age levels and distribution, security level, staff-inmate rapport, the availability of work, training, education, and rehabilitation programs, and housing assignment policies are just a few of these factors. According to the social interaction–demand model, any variable that reduces interpersonal uncertainty, social conflicts, and the intensity of social stimulation should be related to a

reduced impact of institutional crowding. In this chapter, a number of specific suggestions along these lines have been made. It is hoped that future research will be able to evaluate these possibilities.

10. Additional research is required to document the characteristics of those individuals most prone to the negative effects of crowding. Our research has provided some leads, but an intensive study of inmates who appear to have the most problems with living in crowded conditions may provide a clearer picture.

11. Another important gap in our knowledge is the role of explicit coping responses as well as other adjustive reactions in ameliorating reaction to prison crowding (Fleming, Baum, & Singer, 1984). Two different types of coping strategies have been identified, cognitive reevaluation and direct problem-solving (cf. Folkman, 1984). Cognitive reevaluation involves trying to reduce the emotional stress by reevaluating the stressor stimulus as nonthreatening. Direct or problem-solving coping involves direct behavioral attempts to change the stressor situation.

Although the two different coping strategies may often be used simultaneously, situational factors may result in one being predominant over the other. It is often presumed that in situations where individuals have some expectations that direct problem-solving techniques will be successful, these techniques will be employed. When success of such techniques is unlikely, cognitive reevaluation may predominate (cf., Folkman, 1984; Fleming et al., 1984). An interesting possibility is that the different components of the crowding stress stimulus may elicit different types of coping reactions. Interference may be handled best with direct attempts to reduce interference (e.g., setting up formal or informal rules of interaction). Stimulation may be more difficult to handle in a direct problem-solving manner (one often cannot change the number of people in one's housing unit or environment), so one may have to resort to reevaluation of the stimulus (e.g., people), if this is feasible. Attempts may be made to reduce uncertainty, by getting to know the people or the environmental characteristics, or to gain a greater sense of control (e.g., become friends with the right people).

12. One issue that needs to be addressed in future crowding studies is the role of standards of reference in housing satisfaction (Gaes, 1985); that is, in predicting reactions to housing, is the actual level of density or the degree to which the density of one's housing is greater than that of others in the institution most important? For example, if everyone in a prison lives in open dormitories, will the reaction be less negative than if only some of the inmates live in this type of housing? If "relative deprivation" rather than actual density level is found to be most important, improvement in prison conditions may not always be accompanied by favorable reactions, especially with inmates who do not have experience with prior inferior conditions. "Relative deprivation" could also be a partial explanation for the strong reactions we have observed to changes in population within institutions without commensurate changes in facilities.

13. A large number of theoretical issues also remain to be resolved. We need to examine those crowding-related conditions that contribute to uncertainty, interference, and cognitive load. Such research would require the development of ways in which the independent role of these variables can be measured. The degree of unique influence of these variables on the emotional states of fear and anxiety, frustration, and cognitive strain also needs to be demonstrated. The role of each of these emotional states in the various psychological, physiological, and behavioral outcomes needs to be assessed. Such studies would enable one to determine whether uncertainty, in fact, is most important for somatic reactions and interference and cognitive load for psychological reactions. In other words, even though our results give plausibility to the social interaction–demand perspective, the precise relationships implied by the model await verification by studies explicitly designed to assess these relationships.

In summary, the project has provided much useful data of both a pragmatic and theoretical nature. Future studies will need to assess the generality of these findings in other environments and will have to assess specifically the underlying processes that have been posited as being responsible for the observed relationships.

This volume has focused primarily on the psychological effects of living in crowded prison conditions. Our studies represent only one aspect of the scholarly literature on prison crowding. Some scholars have focused on the societal and legal factors that influence population levels in prisons (cf. Gottfredson & Gottfredson, 1986). These projections generally suggest that prison populations will continue to rise. Most projections have thus far underestimated the growth of prison population. The results of past and future prison crowding research will continue to provide an objective basis for decisions by officials (judges, standards committees, and prison designers) who help determine prison housing standards and conditions. Another set of scholars has examined the efficacy of various strategies available for reducing prison populations such as early release and victim compensation (Austin & Krisberg, 1985; Austin, 1986). The evidence that prison crowding can lead to considerable pathology provides strong support for the desirability of such strategies. Although many inmates may deserve or need to be incarcerated, alternative policies may be quite appropriate for some types of criminals and, in the process, may reduce the overcrowding problem. While incarceration is likely to remain a major approach in dealing with violators of the law, there appear to be many more economic and effective alternatives to our crime problem than continuing to confine ever larger numbers of inmates in crowded housing in large prisons. In cases where large numbers of inmates continue to be housed in densely populated prisons, our research findings provide a potentially fertile basis for developing environmental and institutional procedures to minimize the impact of crowded living conditions.

Appendix

Questionnaire

NAME _____ NUMBER _____

In this questionnaire you will be asked to use several rating scales. Below is an example of how these scales are used. This particular example involves rating today's weather.

Example: *Today's Weather*

Good	___	_×_	___ :	___ :	___	___	___	Bad
Cold	___	___	___ :	_×_ :	___	___	___	Hot
Comfortable	___	___	___ :	___ :	___	___	_×_	Uncomfortable

In this example someone has checked the blanks to indicate that he thinks that today's weather is pretty good, neither hot nor cold, but very uncomfortable.

All of the questions below will be like the example. The more strongly you feel that the word at one end of the scale (good, cold, etc.) describes how you feel, the closer you should place your check mark toward that end of the scale.

The room, cubicle, cell, or dormitory in which you live.

Good	___ : ___ : ___ : ___ : ___ : ___ : ___		Bad
Unattractive	___ : ___ : ___ : ___ : ___ : ___ : ___		Attractive
Right number of people	___ : ___ : ___ : ___ : ___ : ___ : ___		Too Many People
Unpleasant	___ : ___ : ___ : ___ : ___ : ___ : ___		Pleasant
Well Arranged	___ : ___ : ___ : ___ : ___ : ___ : ___		Poorly Arranged
Uncomfortable	___ : ___ : ___ : ___ : ___ : ___ : ___		Comfortable

Each pair of words that follows describes a feeling. You may generally feel more one way than the other. So, for each pair put a check mark to show how you felt most of the time this past week. The more strongly you feel that the word at the end of the line describes how you feel, the closer you should place your check mark toward that end of the line. Please take your time.

This past week most of the time I felt

Relaxed	____:____:____:____:____:____:____	Bored
Wide-Awake	____:____:____:____:____:____:____	Sleepy
Happy	____:____:____:____:____:____:____	Unhappy
Tough	____:____:____:____:____:____:____	Weak
Satisfied	____:____:____:____:____:____:____	Unsatisfied
Stimulated	____:____:____:____:____:____:____	Relaxed
Important	____:____:____:____:____:____:____	Unimportant
Tense	____:____:____:____:____:____:____	Calm

In control
  of my situa-
  tion in this
  institution ____:____:____:____:____:____:____ Not in control of my situation in this institution

In control
  over others
  in this
  institution ____:____:____:____:____:____:____ Not in control over others in this institution

Questionnaire

NAME _____ NUMBER _____ BIRTHDATE ____

1. How much more time do you expect to serve?

   _____

2. Date arrived at institution

   _____

3. Have you even been in prison before? If yes, where and for how long?

   Prison or Jail   *How Long*

   _____   _____

   _____   _____

   _____   _____

4. Job assignment in this prison

   _____

5. Level of custody at this prison

   _____

6. Listed below are prison activities. Do you do any of them? How many times a week?

Activities	Yes	Times Per Week
Sports	____	_____
Religious	____	_____
Clubs	____	_____
Education	____	_____
Other	____	_____

7. Do you have any trouble sleeping?
   Never _____ Occasionally _____ Often _____
8. Do you have problems with headaches?
   Never _____ Occasionally _____ Often _____
9. As a child did you live in a small town of 30,000 or less or a larger city?

   _____

10. As an adult have you lived most of your life in a small town of 30,000 or less or a larger city?

    _____

11. While you were growing up how many people, including yourself, lived in your home?

    _____

12. How would you rate your home life while you were growing up?
    Excellent ____ Good ____ Fair ____ Poor ____ Very Poor ____
13. How much time do you typically spend talking to people?
    A great deal ____ Quite a bit ____ A little ____ Very Little ____

14. Father: Occupation _____ Did he complete High School? _____
15. Mother: Occupation _____ Did she complete High School? _____
16. What are some things that bother you most about your housing conditions?

_____

17. If you had to choose, what would you say bothers you most, too many people in your cell or too little space in your cell?

    Check one: Too many people _____

                 Too little space _____

18. How much choice do you think you have about where you live in this prison?

A whole		Pretty	A little	Not at
lot _____	A lot _____	much _____	bit _____	all _____

19. How much choice do you think you have about whom you live with in this prison?

A whole		Pretty	A little	Not at
lot _____	A lot _____	much _____	bit _____	all _____

20. How much say do you think you have in how this prison is run?

A whole		Pretty	A little	Not at
lot _____	A lot _____	much _____	bit _____	all _____

21. How much choice do you have over whether you can do the recreational activities you like to do in this prison?

A whole		Pretty	A little	Not at
lot _____	A lot _____	much _____	bit _____	all _____

22. What type of housing would you prefer in your unit?

    Open dormitory _____ Double cell _____ Single cell _____

References

Aiello, J.R., Baum, A., & Gormley, F.P. (1981). Social determinants of residential crowding stress. *Personality and Social Psychology Bulletin, 7*, 643–649.

Aiello, J.R., Epstein, Y.M., & Karlin, R.A. (1975). Effects of crowding on electrodermal activity. *Sociological Symposium, 14*, 42–57.

Altman, I. (1975) *The environment and social behavior.* Monterey, CA: Brooks/Cole.

American Correctional Association (1981). *Standards for adult correctional institutions* (2nd ed.). College Park, MD: American Correctional Association.

Austin, J. (1986). Using early release to relieve prison crowding: A dilemma in public policy. *Crime and Delinquency, 32*, 404–502.

Austin, J., & Krisberg, B. (1985). The extent and future of imprisonment. *The Annals, 478*, 15–30.

Baron, R.A. (1977). *Human aggression.* New York: Plenum Press.

Baron, R.M., Mandel, D.R., Adams, C.A., & Griffen, L.M. (1976). Effects of social density in university residential environments. *Journal of Personality and Social Psychology, 34*, 434–446.

Baron, R.M., & Rodin, J. (1978). Personal control as a mediator of crowding. In A. Baum, J.E. Singer, & S. Valins (Eds.), *Advances in environmental psychology* (pp. 145–190). Hillsdale, NJ: Erlbaum.

Baum, A., & Koman, S. (1976). Differential response to anticipated crowding: Psychological effects of social and spatial density. *Journal of Personality and Social Psychology, 34*, 526–536.

Baum, A., & Paulus, P.B. (1987) Crowding. In D. Stokols & I. Altman, (Eds.), *Handbook of environmental psychology* (Vol. 1), (pp. 533–570). New York: Wiley.

Baum, A., & Valins, S. (1977). *Architecture and social behavior: Psychological studies of social density.* Hillsdale, NJ: Erlbaum.

Baum, A., & Valins, S. (1979). Architectural mediation of residential density and control: Crowding and the regulation of social contact. In L. Berkowitz (Ed.), *Advances in experimental social psychology* (Vol. 12), (pp. 131–175). New York: Academic Press.

Bonta, J. (1986). Prison crowding: Searching for the functional correlates. *American Psychologist, 41*, 99–101.

Booth, A., & Cowell, J. (1976). Crowding and health. *Journal of Health and Social Behavior, 17*, 204–220.

Booth, A., & Welch, S. (1973). *The effects of crowding: A cross-national study.* Unpublished manuscript, Ministry of State for Urban Affairs, Ottawa, Canada.

Brayton, A.R., & Brain, P.F. (1974). Studies of the effects of differential housing on some measures of disease resistance in male and female laboratory mice. *Journal of Endocrinology, 61,* XLVIII–XLIX.

Bruehl, D., Horvat, G., & George, G. (1979). *Population density and institutional performance in a treatment unit at the Federal Correctional Institution at Terminal Island, California.* Paper presented at the Academy of Criminal Justice Sciences Annual Meeting, Cincinnati, OH.

Bukstel, L.H., & Kilmann, P.R. (1980). Psychological effects of imprisonment on confined inmates. *Psychological Bulletin, 88,* 469–493.

Calhoun, J.B. (1962). Population density and social pathology. *Scientific American, 206,* 139–148.

Calhoun, J.B. (1970). Space and the strategy of life. *Ekistics, 29,* 425–437.

Calhoun, J.B. (1973). Death squared: The explosive growth and demise of a mouse population. *Proceedings of the Royal Society of Medicine, 66,* 80–88.

Carr, T.S. (1980). *The effects of crowding on recidivism, cardiovascular deaths, and infraction rates in a large prison system.* Unpublished doctoral dissertation, Georgia State University, Atlanta.

Cholden, H., & Roneck, D. (1975, April). *Density and pathology: The issue expanded.* Paper presented at the meeting of the Population Association of America, Seattle.

Christian, J.J. (1963). The pathology of overpopulation. *Military Medicine, 128,* 571–603.

Christian, J.J., & Davis, D.E. (1964). Endocrines, behavior and population. *Science, 146,* 1550–1560.

Cohen, S., Glass, D.C., & Phillips, S. (1979). Environment and health. In H.E. Freeman, S. Levine, & L.G. Reeder (Eds.), *Handbook of medical sociology* (pp. 134–149). Englewood Cliffs, NJ: Prentice-Hall.

Collette, J., & Webb, S.D. (1975). *Urban density, crowding and stress reactions.* Unpublished manuscript, University of Utah, Salt Lake City.

Cox, V.C., Paulus, P.B., & McCain, G. (1984). Prison crowding research: The relevance for prison housing standards and a general approach regarding crowding phenomena. *American Psychologist, 39,* 1148–1160.

Cox, V.C., Paulus, P.B., & McCain, G. (1986). Not for attribution: Reply to Bonta. *American Psychologist, 41,* 101–103.

Cox, V.C., Paulus, P.B., McCain, G., & Karlovac, M. (1982). The relationship between crowding and health. In A. Baum & J. Singer (Eds.), *Advances in environmental psychology* (Vol. 4), (pp. 271–294). Hillsdale, NJ: Erlbaum.

Cox, V.C., Paulus, P.B., McCain, G., & Schkade, J.K. (1979). Field research on the effects of crowding in prisons and on offshore drilling platforms. In J.R. Aiello & A. Baum (Eds.), *Residential crowding and design* (pp. 95–106). New York: Plenum.

D'Atri, D.A. (1975). Psychophysiological responses to crowding. *Environment and Behavior, 7,* 237–252.

D'Atri, D.A., Fitzgerald, E.F., Kasl, S.V., & Ostfeld, A.M. (1981). Crowding in prison: The relationship between changes in housing mode and blood pressure. *Psychosomatic Medicine, 43,* 95–105.

D'Atri, D.A., & Ostfeld, A.M. (1975). Crowding: Its effects on the elevation of blood pressure in a prison setting. *Preventive Medicine, 4*, 550–566.

Dabbs, J.M. Jr., Johnson, J.E., & Leventhal, H. (1968). Palmar sweating: A quick and simple measure. *Journal of Experimental Psychology, 78*, 347–350.

Dean, L.M., Pugh, W.M., & Gunderson, E.K.E. (1975). Spatial and perceptual components of crowding: Effects on health and satisfaction. *Environment and Behavior, 7*, 225–236.

Dean, L.M., Pugh, W.M., & Gunderson, E.K.E. (1978). The behavioral effects of crowding: Definitions and methods. *Environment and Behavior, 10*, 419–431.

Desor, J.A. (1972). Toward a psychological theory of crowding. *Journal of Personality and Social Psychology, 21*, 79–83.

Ehrlich, P.R., & Erhlich, A.H. (1970). *Population, resources, environment.* San Francisco: Freeman.

Ekland-Olson, S. (1986). Crowding, social control, and prison violence: Evidence from the post-Ruiz years in Texas. *Law and Society Review, 20*, 389–421.

Elliott, G.R., & Eisdorfer, C. (Eds.). (1982). *Stress and human health.* New York: Springer.

Ellis, D. (1984). Crowding and prison violence: Integration of research and theory. *Criminal Justice and Behavior, 11*, 277–308.

Eoyang, C.K. (1974). Effects of group size and privacy in residential crowding. *Journal of Personality and Social Psychology, 30*, 389–392.

Epstein, Y.M., & Karlin, R.A. (1975). Effects of acute experimental crowding. *Journal of Applied Social Psychology, 5*, 34–53.

Evans, G.W. (1979). Behavioral and physiological consequences of crowding in humans. *Journal of Applied Social Psychology, 9*, 27–46.

Evans, G.W., & Cohen, S. (1987). Environmental stress. In D. Stokols & I. Altman (Eds.), *Handbook of environmental psychology* (Vol. I), (pp. 571–610). New York: Wiley.

Evans, G.W., & Howard, R.B. (1973). Personal space. *Psychological Bulletin, 80*, 334–344.

Farrington, D.P., & Nuttall, C.P. (1980). Prison size, overcrowding, prison violence, and recidivism. *Journal of Criminal Justice, 8*, 221–231.

Fischer, C.S., Baldassare, M., & Ofshe, R.J. (1975). Crowding studies and urban life: A critical review. *Journal of the American Institute of Planners* (Nov.), 406–418.

Flanagan, T.J. (1981). Dealing with long–term confinement. *Criminal Justice and Behavior, 8*, 201–222.

Fleming, R., Baum, A., & Singer, J.E. (1984). Toward an integrative approach to the study of stress. *Journal of Personality and Social Psychology, 46*, 939–949.

Folkman, S. (1984). Personal control and stress and coping processes: A theoretical analysis. *Journal of Personality and Social Psychology, 46*, 839–852.

Franklin, B. (1969). *Autobiography.* New York: Holt, Rinehart and Winston.

Freedman, J.L. (1975). *Crowding and behavior.* San Francisco: W.H. Freeman.

Freedman, J.L. (1979). Reconciling apparent differences between the responses of humans and other animals to crowding. *Psychological Review, 86*, 80–85.

Freedman, J.L., Heshka, S., & Levy, A. (1975). Population density and pathology: Is there a relationship? *Journal of Experimental Social Psychology, 11*, 539–552.

Freedman, J.L., Klevansky, S., & Ehrlich, P.R. (1971). The effect of crowding on human task performance. *Journal of Applied Social Psychology, 1*, 7–25.

Freedman, J., Levy, A.S., Buchanan, R.W., & Price, J. (1972). Crowding and human aggressiveness. *Journal of Experimental Social Psychology, 8,* 528–548.

Gaes, G.G. (1982). *The effect of spatial and architectural housing variations on acute inmate morbidity indicators.* Unpublished manuscript, Office of Research, Federal Prison System, Washington, DC.

Gaes, G.G. (1985). The effects of overcrowding in prison. In M. Tonry & N. Morris (Eds.), *Crime and justice: An annual review of research* (Vol. 6), (pp. 95–146). Chicago: University of Chicago Press.

Gaes, G.G., & McGuire, W.J. (1985). Prison violence: The contribution of crowding versus other determinants of prison assault rates. *Journal of Research in Crime and Delinquency, 22,* 41–65.

Galle, O.R., Gove, W.R., & McPherson, J.M. (1972). Population density and pathology: What are the relations for man? *Science, 176,* 23–30.

Gifford, R. (1987). *Environmental Psychology.* Newton, MA: Allyn and Bacon.

Gottfredson, S.D., & Gottfredson, D.M. (1986). Accuracy of prediction models. In A. Blumstein, J. Cohen, J.A. Roth, & C.A. Visher (Eds.), *Criminal careers and career criminals* (pp. 212–290). Washington DC: National Academy Press.

Gove, W.R., Hughes, M., & Galle, O.R. (1979). Overcrowding in the home: An empirical investigation of its possible pathological consequences. *American Sociological Review, 44,* 59–80.

Henry, J.P., Stephens, P.M., Axelrod, J., & Mueller, R.A. (1971). Effect of psycho-social stimulation on the enzymes involved in the biosynthesis and metabolism of noradrenaline and adrenaline. *Psychosomatic Medicine, 33,* 227–237.

Herzog, A., Levy, L., & Verdonk, A. (1977). Some ecological factors associated with health and social adaptation in the city of Rotterdam. *Urban Ecology, 2,* 205–234.

Hutt, C., & Vaizey, M.J. (1966). Differential effects of group density on social behavior. *Nature, 209,* 1371–1372.

Innes, C.A. (1987). The effects of prison density on prisoners. *Bulletin of the Criminal Justice Archive and Information Network* (Spring), 1–3.

Jacobs, J.B. (1977). *Stateville: The penitentiary in mass society.* Chicago: University of Chicago Press.

Jan, L. (1980). Overcrowding and inmate behavior: Some preliminary findings. *Criminal Justice and Behavior, 7,* 293–301.

Jones, S.E., & Aiello, J.R. (1973). Proxemic behavior of black and white first-, third-, and fifth-grade children. *Journal of Personality and Social Psychology, 25,* 21–27.

Kirmeyer, S.L. (1978). Urban density and pathology. *Environment and Behavior, 10,* 247–269.

Lazarus, R.S., & Folkman, S. (1984). *Stress, appraisal, and coping.* New York: Springer.

Levy, L., & Herzog, A.N. (1974). Effects of population density and crowding on health and social adaptation in the Netherlands. *Journal of Health and Social Behavior, 15,* 228–240.

Loo, C.M. (1972). The effects of spatial density on the social behavior of children. *Journal of Applied Social Psychology, 4,* 372–381.

Loo, C.M. (1978). Density, crowding, and preschool children. In A. Baum & Y.M. Epstein (Eds.), *Human response to crowding* (pp. 371–388). Hillsdale, NJ: Erlbaum.

Loo, C.M., & Ong, P. (1984). Crowding perceptions, attitudes, and consequences among the Chinese. *Environment and Behavior, 16*, 55–87.

Manton, K.G., & Myers, G.C. (1977). The structure of urban mortality: A methodological study of Hanover, Germany, Part II. *International Journal of Epidemiology, 6*, 213–223.

Mason, J.W. (1975). Emotion as reflected in patterns of endocrine integration. In L. Levi (Ed.), *Emotions: Their parameters and measurement* (pp. 143–181). New York: Raven Press.

Matthews, R.W., Paulus, P.B., & Baron, R.A. (1979). Physical aggression after being crowded. *Journal of Nonverbal Behavior, 4*, 5–17.

McCain, G., Cox, V.C., & Paulus, P.B. (1976). The relationship between illness complaints and degree of crowding in a prison environment. *Environment and Behavior, 8*, 283–290.

McCain, G., Cox, V.C., & Paulus, P.B. (1980). *The effect of prison crowding on inmate behavior*. Washington, DC, National Institute of Justice. Available from the Criminal Justice Reference Service, Rockville, MD.

McCain, G., Cox, V.C., Paulus, P.B., & Karlovac, M. (1981). *Social disorganization as a factor in 'crowding'*. Presented at the Midwestern Psychological Association Convention, Detroit.

McCain, G., & Paulus, P.B. (1982). *A preliminary study of crowding in jails*. Washington, DC: National Institute of Justice. Available from the Criminal Justice Reference Service, Rockville, MD.

McKay, H.B., Jayewardene, C.H., & Reedie, P.B. (1979). *The effects of long-term incarceration*. Communication Division, Solicitor General of Canada.

Mechanic, D. (1976). Stress, illness, and illness behavior. *Journal of Human Stress, 2*, 1–6.

Megargee, E.I. (1977). The association of population density, reduced space, and uncomfortable temperatures with misconduct in a prison community. *American Journal of Community Psychology, 5*, 289–298.

Michelson, W.H. (1976). *Man and his urban environment: A sociological approach*. Reading, MA: Addison-Wesley.

Milgram, S. (1970). The experience of living in cities. *Science, 167*, 1461–1468.

Mitchell, R.E. (1971). Some social implications of high density housing. *American Sociological Review, 36*, 18–29.

Myers, K., Hale, C.S., Mykytowycz, R., & Hughes, R.L. (1971). The effects of varying density and space on sociality and health in animals. In A.H. Esser (Ed.), *Behavior and environment: The use of space by animals and men* (pp. 148–187). New York: Plenum.

Nacci, P.L., Teitelbaum, H.E., & Prather, J. (1977). Population density and inmate misconduct rates in the federal prison system. *Federal Probation, 41*, 26–31.

Paulus, P.B. (1980). Crowding. In P.B. Paulus (Ed.), *Psychology of group influence* (pp. 245–289). Hillsdale, NJ: Erlbaum.

Paulus, P.B. (1984). *Effects of crowding and confinement on inmates*. Washington, DC: National Institute of Justice.

Paulus, P.B., Annis, A.B., Seta, J.J., Schkade, J.K., & Matthews, R.W. (1976). Density does affect task performance. *Journal of Personality and Social Psychology, 34*, 248–253.

Paulus, P.B., Cox, V., McCain, G., & Chandler, J. (1975). Some effects of crowding in a prison environment. *Journal of Applied Social Psychology, 5*, 86–91.

Paulus, P.B., & Gaes, G.G. (1986). *Prison housing and the nature of illness complaints*. Unpublished manuscript, University of Texas at Arlington, Arlington.

Paulus, P.B., & Matthews, R.W. (1980). When density affects task performance. *Personality and Social Psychology Bulletin, 6*, 119–124.

Paulus, P.B., & McCain, G. (1983). Crowding in jails. *Basic and Applied Social Psychology, 4*, 89–107.

Paulus, P.B., McCain, G., & Cox, V. (1973). A note on the use of prisons as environments for investigation of crowding. *Bulletin of Psychonomic Society, 1*, 427–428.

Paulus, P.B., McCain, G., & Cox, V.C. (1978). Death rates, psychiatric commitments, blood pressure, and perceived crowding as a function of institutional crowding. *Environmental Psychology and Nonverbal Behavior, 3*, 107–116.

Paulus, P.B., McCain, G., & Cox, V.C. (1985). The effects of crowding in prisons and jails. In D.P. Farrington and J. Gunn (Eds.), *Reactions to crime: The public, the police, courts, and prisons* (pp. 113–134). London: Wiley.

Porporino, F.J., & Dudley, K. (1984). *An analysis of the effects of crowding in Canadian penitentiaries*. Ottawa: Research Division, Programs Branch, Ministry of Solicitor General of Canada.

Rhodes v. Chapman, 101 S. Ct. 2392 (1981).

Rodin, J. (1976). Density, perceived choice and response to controllable and uncontrollable outcomes. *Journal of Experimental Social Psychology, 12*, 564–578.

Rohe, W., & Patterson, A.H. (1974). *The effects of varied levels of resources and density on behavior in a day care center*. Paper presented at the meetings of the Environmental Design Research Association, Milwaukee, WI.

Ross, M., Layton, B., Erickson, B., & Schopler, J. (1973). Affect, facial regard, and reactions to crowding. *Journal of Personality and Social Psychology, 28*, 69–76.

Ruback, R.B., & Carr, T.S. (1984). Crowding in a women's prison: Attitudinal and behavioral effects. *Journal of Applied Social Psychology, 14*, 57–68.

Ruback, R.B., Carr, T.S., & Hopper, C.H. (1986). Perceived control in prison: Its relation to reported crowding, stress, and symptoms. *Journal of Applied Social Psychology, 16*, 375–386.

Ruiz v. Estelle, 503 F. Supp. 1265, 1278 (S.D. Tex. 1980).

Russell, G. (1984). People, people, people. *Time*, August 6.

Saegert, S.C. (1974). *Effects of spatial and social density on arousal, mood, and orientation*. Unpublished doctoral dissertation, University of Michigan, Ann Arbor.

Saegert, S. (1978). High-density environments: Their personal and social consequences. In A. Baum & Y.M. Epstein (Eds.), *Human response to crowding* (pp. 257–281). Hillsdale, NJ: Erlbaum.

Saegert, S. (1982). Environment and children's mental health: Residential density and low income children. In A. Baum & J.E. Singer (Eds.), *Handbook of psychology and health* (Vol. 2) (pp. 247–271). Hillsdale, NJ: Erlbaum.

Sales, S.M., Guydosh, R.M., & Iacano, W. (1974). Relationship between "strength of the nervous system" and the need for stimulation. *Journal of Personality and Social Psychology, 29*, 16–22.

Schaeffer, M.A., Paulus, P.B., Baum, A., & Gaes, G.G. (in press). Architecturally mediated effects of social density in prison. *Environment and Behavior*.

Schmitt, R.C. (1966). Density, health, and social disorganization. *American Institute of Planners Journal, 32,* 38–40.

Selye, H. (1956). *The stress of life.* New York: McGraw-Hill.

Smith, D.L. (1977). *Adult male suicide in the correctional setting.* Unpublished master's thesis, Sam Houston State University, Huntsville, TX.

Stokols, D. (1972). On the distinction between density and crowding: Some implications for future research. *Psychological Review, 79,* 275–277.

Stokols, D. (1976). The experience of crowding in primary and secondary environments. *Environment and Behavior, 8,* 49–86.

Stokols, D., Rall, M., Pinner, B., & Schopler, J. (1973). Physical, social and personal determinants of the perception of crowding. *Environment and Behavior, 5,* 87–115.

Wener, R., & Keys, C. (1986). *The effects of changes in jail population densities on crowding, sick call, and spatial behavior.* Unpublished manuscript, Polytechnic Institute of New York, New York.

Winsborough, H.H. (1965). The social consequences of high population density. *Law and Contemporary Problems, 30,* 120–126.

Wohlwill, J., & Kohn, I. (1973). The environment as experienced by the migrant: An adaptation level view. *Representative Research in Social Psychology, 4,* 135–164.

Zillman, D. (1979). *Hostility and aggression.* Hillsdale, NJ: Erlbaum.

Zlutnick, S., & Altman, I. (1972). Crowding and human behavior. In J.F. Wohlwill & D.H. Carson (Eds.), *Environment and the social sciences: Perspectives and applications* (pp. 44–58). Washington, DC: American Psychological Association.

Author Index

Subject Index